One thousand suns sleeping with the
smile of the Beloved

mpT
MODERN POETRY
IN TRANSLATION
The best of world poetry

No.2 2016
© *Modern Poetry in Translation* 2016 and contributors

ISSN (print) 0969-3572
ISSN (online) 2052-3017
ISBN (print) 978-1-910485-11-8
ISBN (ebook) 978-1-910485-12-5

Editor: Sasha Dugdale
Managing Editor: Deborah de Kock
Web and Communications Manager: Ed Cottrell
Design by Katy Mawhood
Cover art by Emanuel Tegene

Printed and bound in Great Britain by Charlesworth Press, Wakefield
For submissions and subscriptions please visit www.mptmagazine.com

Modern Poetry in Translation Limited. A Company Limited by Guarantee
Registered in England and Wales, Number 5881603
UK Registered Charity Number 1118223

 Supported using public funding by
ARTS COUNCIL
ENGLAND

Modern Poetry in Translation is proud to be a partner of the
Winchester Poetry Festival   www.winchesterpoetryfestival.org

MODERN POETRY IN TRANSLATION

One Thousand Suns

CONTENTS

Focus

Reviews

If you've been with us this year, celebrating our fiftieth anniversary, you'll know that, together with Bloodaxe Books, we published an anthology of poems called *Centres of Cataclysm* and we held launches and study days in Oxford and Cambridge. We made new friends, published new poets and translators, recorded podcasts of poems from around the world, published blogs, education packs, translation workshops, articles, posts.

Over the year we published experimental, lyrical, formal, political and prose poetry, poetry from Old English and modern Persian, ancient Chinese and performance poetry. We published radical translations, translations of great faithfulness, by both acclaimed and expert translators and poets new to translation. We published poems from nearly a hundred languages and by hundreds of poets, we typeset and proofed tens of thousands of words and had correspondences with poets around the world.

We had readings in London, Paris, Oxford, Brighton, Edinburgh, we spoke and read poems in schools, libraries, colleges and community centres to retired poetry-lovers and teenagers who needed winning round and who were won round. We supported refugees with a special refugee issue and with royalties from our anthology, and we distributed the children's issue 'I WISH…' to schools across the UK, together with materials for introducing the poems to young children. We also built a whole new website dedicated to the very first issue in 1965 www.modernpoetryintranslation.com and peopled it with poets and poems. Who says poetry makes nothing happen?

As we did all this (and I mean *all of us* – we did it with the support, encouragement and participation of our many, many good friends, our contributors, hosts, readers and audiences from

'the civilising power of poetry'

Fergal Keane

The very first issue of *Modern Poetry in Translation* is
now online at www.modernpoetryintranslation.com

all around the world) other people bombed hospitals and towns, they raped, mutilated and killed in the most frightful ways, they firebombed shops and chanted hateful things, they knifed and ran over strangers, they trafficked refugees and migrants and in doing so killed them. They sold lifejackets to children that absorb water and sink, they spoke against refugees and the poor, they set up walls and chains of soldiers and riot police. They bullied, they lied, they made promises they couldn't keep and they cheated. They were racist and encouraged hate crimes, they sent aggressive and frightening tweets, they bluffed, threatened and bribed. In the summer of 2016 our human dignity lies around us in tatters.

It has been a shock for some of us to look round and see with such sudden sharpness that personal articles of faith (a belief in internationalism, in hospitality, in the importance of other cultural expressions and ways of being and in the common humanity that underpins them) are actually inimical to others. Now we, too, are eaten away by bitter impotence and the sense of some irrevocable change in the state of the world. 2016 is a bereavement of a year.

We might consider it a privilege to have got this far without the intrusion of such a grave political-existential crisis – our friends from other parts of the world have grown up with this sense of alienation and powerlessness and it is clearer than ever now how they have dealt with it. When I read poets like Golan Haji or Choman Hardi, Kim Hyesoon or Recaredo Silebo Boturu (in this issue) I see they have elected to put their faith in what Fergal Keane at a recent MPT reading called 'the civilising power of poetry'.

Sasha Dugdale

Shortly after completing a translation of the medieval dream-elegy *Pearl*, I discovered Martinus Nijhoff's 1934 poem *Awater* in David Colmer's recent translation for Anvil, and was struck by the consonances between the two. In Nijhoff's echoing and enigmatic poem the narrator, searching for a substitute for his late brother, stalks a mysterious figure named Awater through the city streets at night. Elegiac and allusive, the two narratives six centuries apart pursue their different fugitive dream-guides only to each discover the impossibility of joining them, although they are powerfully drawn to follow them.

Deliberately invoking an old European form to explore the very modern existential questions at the heart of *Awater*, Nijhoff takes as his model the *Chanson de Roland's* 'laisse-monorime', playing on only 8 different vowel-rhymes across nearly 300 lines. The effect is haunting and hypnotic, and it's a form I found propelling as 'The Occupant' came into being while I recorded interviews with *Awater* admirers as part of a recent Netherlands residency hosted by the Dutch Foundation for Literature. These recordings can be heard online on the Poetry Society's Soundcloud site.

Hailed by Brodsky as 'the future of poetry', Martinus Nijhoff's *Awater* is the great Dutch modernist poem, yet it is hardly known outside the Netherlands.

Jane Draycott will be reading 'The Occupant' at a 'European Voices' event at the Winchester Poetry Festival on 8 October 2016. Book tickets via www.winchesterpoetryfestival.org

The Occupant

... alsof hij hoort waarvan hij droomt
en de plek ziet waar hij te vinden hoopt

... as though he hears the thing he's dreamed of
and sees the place he'd hoped to find

– Martinus Nijhoff, *Awater*

And so because I cannot sleep I leave
the hothouse of my sheets
and walk the streets. How close to me
right now are you? The dead lanes keep
their silence, well-trained in secrecy.
The air's like silk, the trees and street-lamps
only like themselves. No dream
could say it clearer. Some compass needle
leads me to the park, where gates of steel
declare '*Each plant and planet feels*
the inmost drive to move and dream.'
A young man lies here on a bench, beached
on the night's cool sand – his breathing
falters as I pass. The place is feverish
with noise. A sign' Menagerie'
directs me to the regions deep
inside the body of the city,
my ears a stethoscope to its squeals
and ticks, its troubled moans and shrieks.

In their concrete yard the camels' feet
enact some pilgrimage across a sweep
of long-lost dunes, the gilded eagle
listens for the wind-scoured fields
and in the keeper's office floorboards creak
remembering their former life at sea.
Only the dogs and last night's heat
lie quiet now, their histories deleted.
That's what I'd like my life to be,
not the dream but the young man sleeping.

II

All day becalmed the city sits
at anchor. In Victory Gardens tourists
cram the shady benches, jasmine
shrivels in the back streets, at tills
and kiosks police post notices,
Missing: Have you seen this wind?
The frail expire and pale dogs whimper,
quarantined on this stilled ship.

Just now I thought I saw you slip
a needle's eye through tram doors, singing
as you went. Only that glimpse
and you were gone, invisible,
eclipsed once more by stone and brick.
The heat patrols the precinct,
windows, walls and doorways frisked
in turn. The sun's eye never blinks.

I pray for a miraculous pitch
of snow. Across the road a cinema
beckons, EXIT-WAY IN
the doors revolve, *this way for winter*
they seem to say. It's like a fridge
in here, the inside of a kiss
made cool by ice and gin. I swim
into its darker water, swallowed in.

The film's set in some future city –
narrowed skies, the air electric,
a chase scene through a crowd spilled out
across a pavement late-night drinking.
And then I see you there amid
the extras, as if you'd walked in
from the street and been uplifted
to the screen, its living window.

You seem so happy there. What is
that world? So much I'd never noticed
I see now – how tall and willowy
you've grown, the way your spirit flickers
between eyes and lips. Film
does that, the focus on the face, the skin.
Outside it's getting dark. A stirring's
in the air, a breath from somewhere distant
as though a storm had flapped a wing.

III

Boarding the tram was like taking my place
on the back of the mythical serpent, that tale

of citizens carried along the lanes
in open daylight, watched from gables

and roof-lights by neighbours who gazed
amazed as the dragon snaked them away.

'Better to travel than arrive,' you always say
so I sing to keep my spirits raised.

We have come to a region of skyscrapers,
giant redwoods of glass that sway

under the clouds. We have come to a place
I never dreamed so close, so strange.

It seems like forever. We are going to tame
the storm and sea. I cannot wait.

IV

Raised on the storm-farm he roams
the horizon, lamplighter far from home
powering through cloud's blown
sail, close to overload. Some woeful
wrong-doing done, some woe
to raise electrodes in the throat.

Then, cinema inferno,
white water solders
down the sky's sheer stone
and rain comes molten.
Furious now he throws
it all in the fire-pit. So
the house blows wholly open.

Our street's a shallow sound, water no wider
than a child might wade to cross its sudden tide.
The city falling shivers on its shine
and in our rows of lighthouses we climb
the stairs to keep the lantern rooms alight.
Where in all this rain are you? The grapevine
says you're sleeping out in fields at night,
miles from these dogs and sirens. Beside
the presidential palace some imp or sprite
left over from the storm is tugging wildly
at the flag like a looter in a riot. This time
last year it fluttered at half-mast – *Like a giant
bending low*, you said and wiped
away a tear for whoever must have died.
Perhaps, you said, *the family are at the graveside
now or making tea at home*, and I replied
At times like this some people like to be outside,
not shut up in their cockpit of a fire-tower
in case tonight should be the night
(and this is in a dream) you cycle by
and wave to me across the stream's divide.

I'll wait until the dogs bark five more times
and five more cars – our ministers, scientists,
generals – roll down the palace drive,
then ride out to the dunes and find you
lying in the fine long grasses, fine for miles.
The restless grasses, restless, moving, fine.

JAN WAGNER

Translated by Iain Galbraith

The skill and effectiveness of Jan Wagner's use of a wide range
of poetic forms is often noted. Had I wanted to demonstrate this
quality of his work I might have tried a sonnet, a villanelle, a sestina
or a Sapphic ode. But whether or not the following handful of
translations gives any impression of his formal dexterity ('hawthorn'
is a sequence of haiku, 'lamentation with a yak' shows his flexible
use of syllabics, while 'jonah' displays his fondness for smudgy
rhyme), there is much else that could be said about his poems, which
may be stories, visits to places, encounters with historical figures, or
views of paintings, and which, following different routes, collectively
engage in a dialogue with language itself. 'lamentation with a yak'
is an instance of Wagner's delight in a primitive function of poetry:
it is as if he had discovered a lost trove of magical codes for primary
naming, for those barely traceable processes (ambush, whisper,
adaptation) that once gave us – and continue to give us – words for
things and relationships. Or as if each thing (in the broadest possible
sense) had its own language, and the poet were able to pick up and
body forth its peculiar mode of address. Wagner's books are full
of invitations to take our readerly part in the way things have their
say, and in the exchange whereby they leave their signature in the
sounds, shape and gesture of a poem. His 'Contents' pages name a
wealth of such 'things': 'maize', 'earthworms', 'gecko', 'mushrooms',
'fennel', 'jellyfish', 'shepherd's pie', 'hops', 'see-saw', 'meteorite', 'nail',
'quince jelly', 'tea-bag', 'cabbage', 'silk', 'the catkin' and so forth.
To these, add recent poems such as 'lamentation with a yak', or
'hawthorn', or even 'the captains'. Many of these titles suggest the
potential of bodily exchange (as does 'jonah'), whether by eating
or, in one poem, getting the eponymous 'catkin' stuck up your
nose. 'lamentation with a yak' conjures the animal from a plexus of

syllables sharing and generating the sound of its name, words that give voice to the yak's arduous life and environment. The English contains almost exactly the same number of yakish sounds and syllables as the German, also imitating the German's wider aura of 'a' and 'ach' syllables. It might fairly be countered that English does not use German's interjectionary 'ach' as an expression of lament, and even in Scots it is more likely to imply irritation or impatience. All I can say in my defence is that I do use it (rather than alas, ah, or o dear – who wouldn't?) and that, anyway, this is also a German yak.

Iain Galbraith and Jan Wagner will be reading from these new poems at a 'European Voices' event at the Winchester Poetry Festival on 8 October 2016. Book tickets via www.winchesterpoetryfestival.org

lamentation with a yak

he'll drag a mountain up the pass –
pack crammed with silk and sacks of rice;
along the ridge he'll never slack,
slip or stumble – forward always,
never back; past the plane wreck, past
a yeti's spoor in his ladakh
of snow-white mountain stacks: the yak.

his shaggy hair, the shaman's head...
and on his tongue a smack of milk
so fat he'll never lack for grass;
hard to watch a draft beast racked so –
up tracks, through icy cataracts.
pupils as black as lacquer, and
deep within, that feeble glow: ach.

by night the bivouacs, the fires
crackling, fuelled by his sun-baked dung,
smoke carrying across the valley;
by night the arctic chill, the sparkle
of stars, the cracking glaciers, while
his massive skull keeps watch from
the gable of this shack, but ach,
but ach, yak, ach, yak, ach.

hawthorn

hawthorn, a local
snow that never fails to fall,
then falls without end;

the way it begins
in may along the edges
of fields and meadows,

a fragrant blizzard
no mere weather satellite
could ever capture;

bushes, perfect globes,
like the ones they make from glass
and sell as knick-knacks,

where – when the flurry
of snowflakes ends – you can see
the newlyweds stood

in front of a church,
while a tiny train steams past
on the horizon.

to jonah

now and then a light-spill seems to trickle
downward, filtered by baleen it could be dawn
up there, you think; you hear angelic
hordes of ravening gulls, while a throng

of mackerel skitters in, a shoal of sardines;
you hear the surf, a sail, then a hailing voice.
sometimes you note a fragrance, as of pines,
or is it just the memory of that fragrance?

odd the way you cannot dodge your guilt,
no matter whether you blast a town with pollutions
or threat of demise, or, on your own, take flight,
going overboard like a sack of rotten onions.

to feel some weather, cold, or sleet,
just a breath of wind – not this fetid lull,
or that spying eye, bigger than a plate,
which even here, through the thick wall

of blubber and oil, seems only to deride
your shortcomings: like a torch the glowing
sea-sparkle illuminates your cramped plight.
but don't waste time pining

for when you were a son, brother or nephew,
or fretting whether it's april, march or june.
don't dwell on tarshish, long for nineveh.
just call this whale your home, jonah.

the captains

came ashore in our street
finding bolt-holes in widows' digs,
anchoring in widows' bay,
tall and proud. we kept our distance,
paddling round them warily
in our tiny dugouts.

it was april, and a blossoming fleet
of cherries cast off in the gardens:
but they stayed on, scrubbing the lawn-deck,
shoving their white bow waves
of beards before them.

silent men with fish in their names,
silvery, monosyllabic
mr codd, mr bream, mr spratt –
while we were clamped like mussels
to doors and shutters, big-eared
for madagascar and zanzibar,
swapping words like glass beads:
caulking, brig, tarpaulin…

quiet types too with marinated faces,
bronzed even in autumn when a rush
of sodden hands, lost to the foaming deep,
crashed through hedges on colder nights –
on some holidays you would find
them swaying in winds of gale force
two hundred and eighty BAC.

behind the curtains they're still standing,
but they can't see me see them
from this dark garden, too tiny in their sea.

Translated by Margaret Jull Costa

Ana Luísa's poems are resolutely female, but she casts her net very wide
in terms of subject matter: from tender poems about her daughter to
thoughts provoked by finding a crumb lodged in the pages of a second-
hand book to musings about Galileo, the theory of relativity and the
larger themes of loneliness, loss, and death. She is a writer immersed in
her own culture, but steeped, too, in the poetry, for example, of Emily
Dickinson and Shakespeare (she has translated the poetry of both), and
in the world of the Bible and the Greek myths. The result is a poetry
that takes equal pleasure in the physical and metaphysical. 'The most
perfect image', for example, is, on one level, an account of the end of a
relationship, but it also takes us through the actual writing of the poem
we are reading, which grows and flows and finally rises phoenix-like
out of the fire of painful experience. I am usually a prose translator,
and one of the great pleasures for me in translating Ana Luísa's poems
from the Portuguese has been the discovery that I don't necessarily
need to understand everything in order to translate, that, as with Emily
Dickinson's poems, certain lines or images can seem utterly opaque and
yet somehow still brim with meaning. The task of the translator is to try,
if possible, to carry that same meaningful opacity into the translation.

Visitations, or a supposedly gentle poem

She entered very gently, my daughter.

The dawn entered with her, but not
quite as gently. Her bare feet
made less noise than my pencil on the page,
but her laughter was louder than my poem.

She climbed, very gently, onto my lap.

The poem, like her, came creeping in, but not
quite as gently, not with the same
gentle urgency. Like a furtive thief
my daughter stole my inspiration,
those lines – almost finished, almost mine.

And here she fell gently asleep,
contented with her crime.

The world torn in two

The world today is only half, cut in two by
my left ear, the sinister side, an infection,
mild and relative, spreads out like a beach.
I listen to the world muffled by soft sand:

the leaves barely trembling and, on the wooden
floor, my shoe: a sensible, barely
burning echo, and the voices
that reach me from the other room: Orpheus calling
to Eurydice.

A world torn in two: the
earth on one side, and the inferno roaring
in imperfect flames of silence.
Or even more torn in two than the old world

that long ago was mine.
From very far away comes a voice:
'Where can she have got to?
It's so late and she's still not back.'

I linger, like Eurydice, over the rupture
caused by this counter-delay of the senses.
Living in this half-heard half-world,
dying in this inferno of tenderness –

the most perfect image

If each morning I were to sweep up the little
needles that fall from this bush onto the ground that
welcomes them, I would have a perfect metaphor for
what led me to fall out of love with you. If each morning
I were to wash this window and, in the dazzling glass, as well as
my reflection, feel the amused gaze of the transparency
of nothingness, I would see that the bush is merely
an inferno, lacking the decasyllable of the flame.
If each morning I were to look at the spider's web adorning
its branches, I would also understand the imperfection that
from May to August corrupts its threads and
dismantles its geometry. And its colour. Even if I saw
this poem as a conclusion, I would notice how its
line grows, unrhymed, into an uncertain,
broken rhythm that flees from my usual me. The slowness of the
wind, of erosion. I would see that my longing belongs to another
web from another time, not from here, and lent itself
to a neuron of mine, a memory that clings stubbornly
to a kind of beauty: the fire from a funeral pyre.
The most perfect image of art. And of farewell.

Intertextualities

Almost microscopic,
a crumb left between the pages of a book
I happen to be reading.

Someone lent me the book,
but not the crumb.
Shrouded in deepest mystery,
it made its first shy appearance
between two solemn paragraphs,
It tangled my thoughts,
broke the (already tenuous) thread of my reading.
Seductive, intriguing.

It made me consider the different levels to be read:
the subject of the book
and the crumb-subject of the reader.

(someone had consumed a sandwich in between consuming
those two paragraphs with their eyes:
turn the page, read two lines
the plot thickens, just when did he or she
get up to make a sandwich
before returning to read the next few lines)

I was left with the crumb,
an unexpected gift from the reader,
and, as a joke or as a possible snack,
I left a crumb of my own,
not a water mark, but a bread mark:
an alternative theme to be deciphered later
at a later reading
by someone else

Translated by Mario Petrucci

Hafez (or 'Hafiz') was a major Persian poet, born in the fourteenth century in Shiraz in Iran. It's clear that Hafez's influence on global culture and consciousness has been significant way beyond the use of his poems as oracle in the Persian-speaking world. He may enjoy cult status as a classic of medieval Persian literature, but he also brings profound and refreshing relevance to the violent sleepwalking that characterises many of our current human crises. Moreover, publishing Hafez in English in the prevailing political climate inevitably highlights topical issues concerning the true breadth and quality of communication between East and West.

The poems presented here are excerpted from a book-length translation entitled *Beloved*, consisting of eighty-one poems selected from Hafez's most potent ghazals. This project highlights the mystic's long-suffering desire for divine union without diminishing the poet's alertness to sensuously secular concerns and literary play.

385

The veil between me and Beloved reality is this dust body.
In death, breath racing, I'll part at last, as if I were vapour.

I've heard in myself freer songs than from the bodily cage.
Eden's rose-beds will assuage me: I'm a bird of that temper.

Nothing material, no fact, traces back to why we were put here
or the *ergo*-urge before that. Sad regret only saps that purpose.

In this arena of time and space, how may I complete a circuit
as inconstant dust, planked shut, among competing elements?

My place is that natural theatre of angels. Why must I wait
down here, caught between worldly ghosts and inebriates?

Don't gawp, then, if this inner heart pours out pure musk.
I'm of that ilk. I share the fate of the musk deer of China.

I quicken, flare, my face a twist of flame rising from its taper.
I try to insist on being elated; but, deeper in, I melt, evaporate.

I resist, believing one may relieve oneself of oneself. Body is
an eclipse – slip behind yourself, until the only light is God's.

403

If chance could walk me, once again, to the Perfect Master's tavern,
I'd scatter all the pious gains of prayer mat and mantle, purposely
 lose them.

If, today, I forged a bright ring in penance – to sound, as the ascetic
does, one sad note – still, tomorrow's wine-house door wouldn't open
 to it.

If I were blessed – as the moth is – with flights of true carelessness,
I'd flutter surely towards that shimmering Face, into its soft drop of light.

If, since my harp's untuned, there's no string in me You can play,
at least, as though I were a flute, cherish me – breathe me into harmony.

I could solicit angelic forms over Yours: what a lapse, how unshapely,
to split myself thus.

 Heart liquefied inside me to blood: I hide the fact.
Since that, my newest consolation has been grief's honed blade.

My ribs never released their small red bird so passionate for You:
yet, in my eyes' wet verges, half-submerged, its secret song was heard.

I flew from body, rid myself of my cage of bones; but even air, ever open,
is just another kind of prison for those who can only fear God's talons.

Beloved: if each hair on this head were itself a head, I'd amass the fleeting
multitude of myself, as if You'd let fall impossible tresses, at Your feet.

437

One glance in my direction, and immediate agonies crumple me.
Then I catch Your look – and again I stretch towards You, abruptly.

What You secrete, deep within, evades me. You won't stride out to
cure me, never inquire into how I fare. Have You even an idea of me?

Riding past, You bump any stumbler into sand. Cast a look over that fast
-moving shoulder, dismount just once – I'll be glad dust along Your Path.

I'll forever keep this hand to Your cloak. Even when death exacts its due,
approach my grave and those sleeping grains will rear up, grope for You.

This love I hold is anguish, a labour of lack. How much longer, life?
You accept these breathless, reckless blasts – yet leave me breath?

That night when I groomed jet locks to extract my heart, Your trove
of cheek became a cup: I found my fill from lips bejewelled with Love.

Yes: I drew You in, sharply, closer than breath or dagger, heart lost among
densely wisping strands. The rest of me followed, abandoned in a final kiss.

You left, without me, for greener plains.
My blood-rust rains came in gouts to gouge and darken their yellow dunes.

Be kind: insist on death, instead, with those who wish You ill. Be sun
to me, an instant, and I'll not fear foe's dead breath, nor coldest hell.

Translated by Lisa Katz

'After the Horror the Act of Poetry' is the opening poem as well as the title of Kosman's first book, published when he was twenty two. The creation of the poem seems to have entailed the murder of the writer in a kind of public spectacle. 'A Small Pillar of Fire' dates from *We Have Reached God*, Kosman's fifth book, published nearly twenty years later. I would like to imagine that the speaker is the same person as in the earlier poem, and that he has matured enough to marry and establish a home. Here, too, a spectacle is enacted. Somehow, the immense fire inside the home, brought in by horses and chariots themselves made of fire, is not horrifying. Rather it is tamed in a sense, something that the pair, likened to Adam and Eve, can 'kindle' together. There's a phallic 'rod' but also soft clouds and a pillow, a tongue. The couple's small pillar of fire perhaps evokes God's passionate but friendly presence in their home. These poems are highly representative of Kosman's fanciful yet serious imagery of creative power and the possibility of domestic, human divinity.

After the Horror the Act of Poetry

And after the horror the act of poetry,
after the scandal of its birth,
what remains are graphic signs upon the earth,
the chalk scars the police drew in a circle around
the position of my gunned-down body, a warm bullet
still quivering on the ground, and a few people
whispering about what happened here,
after the terrifying din, after the audience dispersed.

A Small Pillar of Fire

The house is filled with chariots of fire.
Young steeds of fire have arrived.
On the rug, a giant rod of fire.
Above us, soft white woolly clouds
infused themselves
into a small pillow, a tongue of fire.

Only then did a treetop ascend over us.
A huge wave, a pure cloud as white as a sheet, of fire.
Afterwards, we sat down, my wife, to a feast of fire.
On the plate, like Adam and Eve
we kindled, together, thrilled,
a small pillar, a delicate one, of fire.

Translated by Carol Martin-Sperry

I am interested in the work of Joyce Mansour and her poems of love and desire because I feel she has a unique and passionate voice. The madness of love and sex are described with the shocking imagery and violent fantasies of the insane. She spares us nothing in her fierce brutality, yet there is often a sad and moving sensitivity in her work. Her poems are stark and painful with a frightening obsessive streak of sado-masochism. Her dark and mad world touches something deep within us. Both the writer and the reader need courage as she reveals her visceral feelings.

I have attempted to respect her bare spare style, her precise choice of vocabulary and the simplicity of her rhythms.

Mansour's work seems to be virtually unknown today and deserves a fresh audience. As a twentieth-century female poet her poems are as relevant today as when she wrote them.

UNTITLED 1

I want to sleep side by side with you

Hair intermingled

Genitals linked

Your mouth as a pillow.

I want to sleep back to back with you

No breath to separate us

No words to distract us

No lying eyes

No clothes.

I want to sleep breast to breast with you

Contorted, sweat

Shining from a thousand shudders

Consumed by the insane inertia of ecstasy

Splayed across your shadow

Hammered by your tongue

Dying between your decayed rabbit's teeth

Happy.

UNTITLED 3

Listen to me

Your hands listen to me

Do not close your eyes

My legs remain open

Despite the howling midday light

Despite the flies

Do not refuse my words

Do not shrug your shoulders

Listen to me, my God

I paid my dues

And my prayers are just as good as my neighbour's.

UNTITLED 5

Every night when I am alone

I tell you of my tenderness

And I strangle a flower.

The fire slowly dies down

Diminished by sadness

And butterflies reside

In the mirror where my shadow sleeps.

Every night when I am alone

I read the future in the eyes of the dying

My breath mingles with the blood of owls

And my heart races at a crescendo

With the insane.

Translated by Anita Gopalan

With a career spanning over two decades and six books to his credit, Geet Chaturvedi is one of the most widely read contemporary Hindi authors. His poetry delights the reader with its inner lyrical beauty and playfulness, as well as its sensitivity and sensibility of ideas and imagination.

This sensitivity is reflected in the poem 'The Memory of Now', which is a string of images and impressions, a kind of conversation the poet often holds with his favourite people in his poems, here his favourite being Eduardo Chirinos, the Peruvian poet. The poem was written for Chirinos as a tribute soon after his death. Geet and Chirinos knew each other only through the written word, through poetry and an exchange of emails. Just days before his death, Chirinos wrote a heart-warming email to Geet: 'I try to take advantage of the rare moments in which I feel fine reading and writing...', and mentioned 'Tomorrow (I hope) I will send the PDF...'. It never happened. Theirs was a bond of much warmth and mutual respect. The poem 'Big Papa's Funeral' is based on a teenage memory and the title reminds us of the Marquez novella. With its theme of secret love, the artistic memory of this poem revels in the mundane and the sublime.

The Memory of Now

(For Eduardo Chirinos)

Downstairs I left a candle burning
In its light I'll read a few lines when I return

By the time I returned the candle had burned out
Those few lines had faded like innocence

You walk with me
The way moon walks along with a child sitting in a train window

I stood in the balcony one day
Waved a handkerchief toward the sky

Those who have gone without saying their goodbyes
Will recognize it even from far

In my handkerchief they have left behind their tears
The way early humans left behind their etchings on cave walls

Lyotard said, every sentence is a now
No. Actually it's a memory of now

Every memory is a poem
In our books, the count of the unwritten poems is so much more

Tales of the Sea

1.

In Search of Thirst

A fish lived in water all day, all night, every moment and while she swam she read 'The Much-Loved Poets of Urdu' which glorified love and thirst and she realized this over and over again: that if there's no thirst, there's no love either and one day she jumped out of the waters in search of her thirst.

2.

The Sea

The sea is a lover, most forgiving. Every moment he forgives the waves receding from him and includes them again into him. Love is to let go. Love is also to accept the ones who have returned.

Big Papa's Funeral

After offering flowers we had huddled round the deceased.
Bowing our heads in respect, gazing long at his face.
Many among us felt the corpse's lips flutter momentarily.
Yes, many among us had felt that, but we kept quiet.
One had even waved a finger under his nostrils just to check.

Even weeks after his cremation, people were discussing
How momentarily the corpse's lips had fluttered even after death
An old woman who was no relation whatsoever to him and who
    ran a café
Told me matter-of-factly one day,
I had faith that he'd come, even after death he'd return
To continue his unfinished kiss.
Well, fifty-three years ago when he was a lad of seventeen
Under the broken bulb of a lamp post on a street corner
He had left a girl in the middle of a kiss and run away.

Translated by Diana Manole and Adam J. Sorkin

'i'm sam', begins Nora Iuga's *The Hunchbacks' Bus* (*Autobuzul cu cocoșați*), which I translated with Diana Manole's expert collaboration. The book is a sort of family chronicle centred on sam and his life, much of which is in his head, his not very faithful wife minodora and his brother istovitu (the name means exhausted, worn-out). It's comic, though not often (at least to me) in a laugh-out-loud kind of way; surreal or fantastic at moments, at others ribald, eccentric; perhaps even a little hard to cosy up to, since Iuga keeps everything at an ironic distance, her style rarely lyrical in a traditional sense. The syntax is direct but the imagery teases and surprises; the poetic voice is energetic, even audacious, with a delightful quirkiness.

In the first of five authorial interludes, short monologues in prose, Iuga addresses the reader, '*you might find it hard to believe, but sam actually exists*' (notwithstanding the fact that he's sometimes presented as a dog); and Iuga notes otherwise in 'sam is an angel':

i'm still determined to find out who
sam is and what he does with his little stick

Iuga's world may at times be one of loss, worry, proverbially a dog's life, but it spins away with exhilarating dreamlike absurdity.

As translators, one of our main challenges was to convey the momentum of Iuga's playful style while accurately conveying her diction and imagery. For translators, as for poets, little things can mean a lot. Even on the level of appearance: along with scant punctuation, no uppercase letters appear in the original, so we preserved this convention. We chose the informality of contractions. One petty betrayal: we helped the English-language reader with some commas in direct discourse. Key cultural allusions had to come through clearly, not just a phrase like Kant's 'starry vault above' and 'moral law within' but also references to Romanian customs and daily life.

There were idiosyncratic moments as well. At one point Manole clued me in on the significance of an odd phrase sam screams in minodora's dream:

> come see what a tumbling rock
> has to go through to reach a beautiful stillness.

Iuga, who is a close friend of Diana's, had explained to her in a phone call, 'everything that's alive and moving aims to reach stillness which means eternity, i.e., eternal death, which is beautiful.'

sam introduces himself to his readers

i'm sam
i have a woman with a green leg
and an ear cut off
i have a woman with a shaved head
and long goat-like tits
in the morning when she goes to the market
dogs pee on her leg
and roses bloom
i have a tender and lusty woman
she licks the chocolate from my fingers
and my fingers stiffen in an erection
i'm sam
i also have a hump

my mama gave it to me when she was a camel
as for anything else i have a happy-go-lucky nature
when it rains i feel like going to the movies
but my master puts me on the leash
i'm a wet puppy i bear it in silence
i make small yellow pretzels
and reflect on the good lord

minodora dreams of sam

mama told me:
minodora, stop thinking about sam
when you go to the market
think of bacon, think of cabbage
be a proper woman
what would have been, i asked her
if beethoven hadn't always had a bird
singing in his head?
yeah but beethoven, mama said
picking up the dust rag
and starting to clean the genius's ears
and that's only because i must
write about you
the same way i must sneeze
or yawn
i dreamt of you last night
you had a baby with a cat's head
he was cute as a button
you were screaming your head off
'come see what a tumbling rock

has to go through to reach a beautiful stillness'
it's a big deal
when you forget to cross yourself
before going to sleep

sam, did you pay the water bill, you kept asking

minodora, do you remember
how you used to knock at my hump in the morning
inside it the nile could be heard murmuring
with palm trees and yellow vipers
like women's garters
and the voice of ramses
freshly awoken from sleep
just after dreaming of you
in the triangle of your bikini
where god's eye kept blinking
do you remember how we'd go to work together
how we shared sesame pretzels
and you lifted the night off your eyes a little
sam, did you pay the water bill, you kept asking
you were shy i led you on
i liked your darkness
i waded through it splashing
until i reached the opposite hemisphere
twenty little boys waited there for me
sharpening pencils
they wanted to know what ramses was up to
he's blabbing on the phone i told them

sam is an angel

how much i love
to take out my little stick
and play with it
sam wrote in his fourth-grade
history textbook
fifty years later
sam is an angel hanging down from a branch
he preens his feathers
and bites his lice like a senile monkey
what else do i have to lose but a landscape
maybe only these houses
the bus passes by
they become smaller and smaller
like soup spoons
in the hands of beggars
and if the mailman doesn't come
if minodora doesn't phone me
i'm still determined to find out who
sam is and what he does with his little stick
i meditate i poke my nose into
this soft warm wool
that the sun heaps high on the table
i don't sleep i keep counting
i'm the most helpless text
in this city

and minodora sang ballads for me

i was so happy when i was fifteen
when i wasn't ashamed of my feelings
when i kissed the dog's nose
in front of everyone
and fell in love with mona lisa
my flesh was chaste unripe
like a virgin soil
i ate gooseberries
the apostles came holding sprigs of apple blossoms
and helped me across the railroad tracks
ah those nights with holes
and god's mercy
came and left
people cried at the walls
like dogs peeing
and minodora sang ballads for me
i enjoyed life
i had the starry vault above me
and the moral law within me

MICHALIS GANÁS

Translated by Joshua Barley

Michalis Ganás is a Greek poet and lyricist with a voice that comes straight from the country's Balkan backbone. He was born in the village of Tsamantás in Epirus in 1944, a wild mountainous place on the borders of Albania. When he was four, the circumstances of the Civil War (1946–1949) drove Ganás's family to various Communist-held countries, particularly Hungary, for eight years. The return to their homeland brought them to a house that had almost fallen apart. One by one the twelve members of the family, crammed together in the draughty house, left to seek a better lot. Michalis, eighteen years old, found himself in Athens, where he has lived ever since. He has come to accept the city, even love it, though he cannot shake off his homeland. The ambivalence he feels is elegantly encapsulated in the sonnet 'Down in Haftía lay me to rest', Haftía being the central district of Athens, around Omonia Square. The disorientating changes in society also underlie 'M.G. 1888–1979', where the death of the poet's grandfather is symbolic of the end of a way of life – or perhaps, a way of death: now that a ceiling has been put in, Charon cannot be seen coming down from the rafters, as the old myth goes. Such traditions intrude into Ganás's poetry in much the same way as his homeland does, though he views neither with nostalgia. His work epitomises the challenges, ambiguities and necessities of a traditional society faced with the onslaught of modernity. This is an honest and clear-sounding voice of Greece that is seldom heard. The poems here are taken from his collection *Black Stones*, published in 1980.

Christ is Risen

We had taken the path back home,
April awash in a sea of cotton,
and the more we slipped among the planes,
the more silent they fell, not a wind blew,
but from within me her eyes were watching me,
glistening from the candlelight,
and I was whistling, I remember, Christ is Risen.

The sky which just before was streaked with lightning
returned to a white and sodden sheet.

Her brother, a stone's throw from the spring,
his trousers and water-flask dripping,
'Christ is Risen. How are you doing?' How could he be doing,
dead almost a year now.
He turned to look at us and the land lit up
like someone taking our photograph at night.

M.G. 1888–1979

With a touch of yellow in your nails and your gaze
your craft goes down, water gaping
black beneath.
The house is empty. Outside, the trees
that were planted by your hand.
Tonight and tomorrow night
your crook, cast off in the corner
and your body that doesn't stop defecating.

You won't see him, from the rafters
he'd come down of old, now
they've put a ceiling in and what's there to see
with the lights of your eyes gone out,
besides, he'll come with a pillow
and smother you like a baby in a cot.

If I remember your hand,
in Skodra, in Balaton, in Beloyanni,
your tattered greatcoat, if I remember
your hand that trembled and made the spoon
rattle on the plate and if I remember your feet,
you know, with the uncut nails, the calluses that
my brother took off, I remember, and
the photographs from America
with Vassilis, with Prokopis, dressed to the
nines, all three with partings, in
Boston in Worcester in Framingham, there
where your sons and grandchildren now work out.

Not light or heavy the earth that rests on you.
Mother will come to find us, the
next day she'll take the bus,
black lambs will graze on your tomb,
the house closed up for ages,
the two dogs fed by the neighbours,
strange bread will feed our dogs.

At The River

In time the leaves fell down,
the fruit became horns, what trumpeted
next to me, the water-water,
stone-stone,
death had no path.

The river, cloudless, with slender water-snakes,
shadows of birds, thousands of cicadas.
What was it that stirred! Pebbles in the channel
and the startled rock thrush.
I turned to look. No one.

Only at the edge, murky water,
traces of giant footsteps
and the stones around them drenched.

I just managed to close my ears
the moment he broke into laughter.

Ascension

Footprints in the snow like
a small child's and yet
they weren't, nor of any known
animal, all day long we searched and all
the night with torches, we lost
two in the treacherous gorges, one
we dragged out with ropes and
for what gain, there where end
the firs, and beyond only
the mountain, suddenly the snow untrodden, without
any trace of a struggle or blood.
We sat up till dawn drinking
all the cognac and eating raisins, until
in the light of day we recoiled
at the sight of each other, threw two
flares, they came with helicopters from
below, raised us up, the snow around
untrodden, without any
trace of a struggle or blood.

Down in Haftía Lay Me to Rest

Posters tugging at my sleeve,
Oh Athens, full of beauty contests.
Down in Haftía lay me to rest,
I've paid you rent for twenty years.

In my sleep pass mountains and forests,
nereids swaddled in black clothes.
The grudge I held you, like a mule's,
on what bus did I cease to bear it?

What madness, tell me, raps at my heels
and I leave and tumble like a skittle,
with tavernas and mute playing fields

in my inner being. People,
places, they all look like strangers,
in photos we took at other ages.

Translated by Rachel Tzvia Back

Israel Bar-Kohav, poet and psychologist, was born in 1950 in Israel, the grandson of Russian immigrants to Ottoman Palestine who numbered among the founders of the city of Tel Aviv in the early twentieth century. The author of twelve books of poetry, Bar-Kohav's 2010 collection *Selected Poems 1975–2010*, published in the classics series of the Bialik Institute, places him among the first rank of contemporary poets of Israel. Renowned Israeli novelist Amos Oz has named Bar-Kohav '...one of the finest and most interesting of [Israel's] poets'. Oz writes: 'I have read his poems for years, astonished by his poetical power, the precision of his expression, and the freshness and originality of his language.' Bar-Kohav himself writes that 'Poetry is born out of the festive moment in which the poet intimately engages with the object, or the other, outside himself; poetry is born out of the moment of mourning that other's absence, that object's loss.'

Order of the Day

Slowly the day blossoms in the sky
and on earth no one smiles.
An envoy of evil angels stings our tender skin
like nettle, to remind us
that even the plants do not wish us well.
We pretend that our journey
is immeasurably deep, but we never seek
ourselves in the mirror, we are motherless and we are fatherless
and more than anything else
we are in search of
something.

Soon, Love

1

Attraction is
the body's tilting toward
love

2

We speak of love
and in our throat the truth appears
like a fish
bone

3

Even as we are still talking
the body speaks its piece
like a prophet of truth

4

High tide is the sea's soul
towards where the drowning direct their love

Picasso's Horse

Never will Picasso's horse rest its foot on the ground.
A boy stands near it gazing at an empty world.
Which is the road untaken?
What are the sights trapped in memory?
The map passes between the absence of movement and the gaze,
Frozen in the murky bluish light
What is the horse?
A clue that it was possible to go out into the world
What is the boy?
He who looks beyond the dream's shoulder.

Chronicles of the Days

Ancient is the sea, ancient are the waters,
Ancient is Tethys Ocean beneath our house in Giva'tayim,
Ancient are the pine trees,
Ancient the people wearied by experience.
Ancient are the ministering stars, ancient the angels of destruction, ancient
    the roads, the islands,
Ancient is India, ancient is my father in his death, ancient are the prophets,
    the prophecies,
Ancient is the *Khurban*, ancient is Jerusalem, ancient heaven's tunnels,
Ancient is White Russia, ancient are the people of the bible, ancient
    the Israelites as they cross the sea on dry land into the great desert,
Ancient are the kings, ancient is Hebrew across the river, ancient is The
    Land of Canaan,
And ancient are the minerals in the veins of the hills, in the memory of
    plants growing along the streams,
Ancient are the animals caged in our bodies
screaming for help.

NOTE: The word *Khurban* which means 'destruction' is a reference to the destruction of the First Temple (586 BCE) and the Second Temple (70 CE) in Jerusalem. The word and historical reality of *khurban* evoke the greatest of calamities that befell the Jews, as embodied in these destructions and the resulting exile. The full phrase for the fall of the Temples is *Khurban Ha'bayit* – the Destruction of the House.

Translated by Susanne Höbel

The first time I came across the name of Nora Bossong was about ten years ago, during a translation workshop in Wolfenbüttel. Having come down early for breakfast on the first morning, I looked around for something to read and found a brochure called *New Voices in German Poetry*. I thumbed through it and read a poem here and there, and when I came to those by Nora Bossong, I was moved and impressed. I read the biographical note – she had composed those poems at the age of nineteen – and thought surely this is a name to remember, this is a new voice.

I soon discovered that Nora Bossong had published a first collection of poems, had been shortlisted for a prize and had written and published a novel. In the meantime the list of her awards and prizes as well as her publications has grown to some length. My hunch had been right, this was a new voice, and it would be heard more often.

These poems are taken from her 2011 collection *Sommer vor den Mauern* (Extramural Summer) and a number of them are set in the windswept landscape of Northern Germany, dominated by both the North Sea and the Baltic. Dwellings and people seek shelter behind dykes, trees function as windbreaks. Many churches, built from red brick and in a Gothic perpendicular style, are visible from afar, and their unadorned interiors, backdrop of some of Nora Bossong's poems, create a sombre and austere atmosphere.

Seventh Woman on the Nuns' Balcony

Oppressive darkness, not to be shut off,
outside the wind, slapping over the villages,
Lemmie, Empelde, Bantorf. On the balcony
she had seen Our Lady, she claims, a face,
serene and real, while she herself was singing
'The Splendour of the Earth' by Gryphius.
A universe of blue. A veil made from the universe,
falling over her shoulders, folds covering
low farmhouses, delicate line drawings
all the way to Lemmie. Illuminated country.
... no, no, just fallen asleep, everything just
so early, the writing so small. Apparitions
are better left to southern faiths,
to marble dogmas. Here there will only be
darkness, wind and Lemmie close by.

The Escape of Our Ladies

Into dappled brightness
they escaped. Church light,
grease-painted for the life beyond.
One Lady of Mercy,
one Lady with child,
one formerly with child,
one dying Lady
came falling out of the stone structure,
the kind of dungeon where usually

stepmothers dwell
and discarded witches.
Radiators leaning
against pews,
the plumbers disappeared
into their lunch break. I stayed behind,
the nave swaying in silence.
It was then that a pale
creature, stone-scratched,
shifted, rolled timidly from her hiding-place,
the last in her row:
the pietà,
the dead Jesus rigid in her arms,
and dropped wooden, plunging at my feet –
at *my* feet, Lady Abbess!
I stayed awake late that day,
regarding my toes,
ten small wonders.

Floral Scene with Lady

Somewhat naked, somewhat cool
she must have stood, until such time as someone,
out of mercy or merely to pass the time,
sewed her a coat: The silk from around fifteen
hundred, with a delicate green trim.
Cheeks painted red, she stares
with earnest doll-like gaze out of the glass cabinet.
She is one of the circle of excavated Ladies,
once walled in, deep in a hundred-year sleep.

Before that, she was the pilgrimage pin-up,
in front of her, growing as high as the hedge, the eyes of
sinners who touched her up for protection.
She herself as tired as only wood tires.
Her almighty, mighty, might-be power
only lures locals from round here.
Still, freshly cut flowers are left for her every day,
Roses from the convent garden.

Young Birds

Cold burst in through the skylight, a bird
had crashed into the glass. Walls of sheets,
socks dancing above me, in the middle of the line
the cast-off skin of two legs: a pair of nylons.
My nose wrinkled, held up to the snowdust,
when she pulled me away from the splintered window,
climbed down the stairs, the tub under her arm,
her sideway walk, her cold singing:
If you were a little bird
and had two little wings.
Her shocking blonde hair, her naked face,
she said, *yes, the baby birds fall from their nests,*
one in two at most makes it and learns to fly.
Left lying on the forest floor until the wild boar gets them.
You can go to Syke in autumn and count them,
see how many you'll find.

Translated by Antonia Lloyd-Jones

These four short poems offer a good 'tasting menu' of Polish
poet Tadeusz Dąbrowski's work. Here you'll find several of his
characteristic features: a helpless yet philosophical attitude to the
human condition; vivid scenery, made to serve the poet's purpose;
the influence of his travels to the United States; and the humour
that gives him resilience as he boldly looks life in the face without
ever flinching. As his translator, the challenge for me is to keep his
lightness of touch, which means being equally concise and faithfully
serving his rhythm, line and sentence breaks. His clever echoes
and balanced choice of contrasting words occasionally defy me, but
mostly his poetry is pleasingly willing to be changed into English –
like its author, it travels well.

With poetry it's like this...

With poetry it's like this: you sail out onto the sea,
cast your net, pull it through millions of tons
of water and finally catch a gigantic crab
much the same as you, which says: Can't you do
your bloody fishing somewhere else?

TADEUSZ DĄBROWSKI

The train races: the trees go by...

The train races: the trees go by like the residents
of big cities in the rush hour. The train is barely
moving: the trees go by dumbly like
patients at a mental hospital. The train
stops: the trees pretend to be a wood.

Portrait of a Woman after a Stroke

The left side of her face knows it all by now,
the right one does as well.

It might seem as if there's no understanding
between them.

But when the mobile half says something or laughs,
the other one stubbornly pulls at a corner of the mouth, calling
its rapturous reflection to order.

It looks a bit like tug-of-war
over a precipice.

Reincarnation

In memory of

The black boy has been looking at me for a month
from subway stations and storefront windows, the reward
for finding him is rising and the photo
quality is falling. At the start they were in colour,

now there are copies everywhere squeezed out
of dying toner. Even his name
has become illegible. He's unlucky he was
born black, because the ink destined for him

runs out faster. On the very last print-outs
he looks quite like me.

Translated by J. Kates

Alicia Aza is a poet with a voice I first heard in Serbia because she ranges widely in the world, but a voice distinctively Peninsular Spanish. The thirty poems of her 2010 *Book of Trees*, which was a finalist for the Andalusia Critics award, are rooted in Madrid and Cordoba, while they draw their nourishment from other voices and foreign music. Of the poems represented here, the poet has said, 'I use the image of the tree to get at feelings, to talk about moods through landscape. Hence the tree appears as an object of my lyrical projection.' But elements of romanticism, realism and surrealism do not define her work. My translations of these poems are an arrogant exercise as well as a humbler homage, my first serious attempt to translate from Spanish without a direct collaborator (although with a collaborator in translating Spanish for more thirty years, I'm working on another of Aza's books).

Silver Mimosa

[seductive vanities]

I would be a flowering bush, asleep
the first day of the new spring
sunrise packed with yellow
seductive gold or silky amber
a wind blowing a heavy pervasive
perfume through its branches.
I would infuse their magic petals
with the fulfillment of desires
and the destruction of curses

and the hurricane left by a trail of lust
turns into a tempering breeze
uncovering its tiny blossoms.
I would be brilliant and silent
where the leaves and the wind preach
the sure and inevitable future
with the light touch attended by instants.

Seaside Promise of Olives

Capricious and unconquerable lovers
destroying their desires in the absent
lands of a haunted moon
that drives its shadow
towards the rivers of the North.

We can not imagine other territories
an undulating horizon green and tranquil.
Your hand stealthily breaking
the white routines
in streets lined with iron grills.

And to feel that if other seas exist
acceptable into new memory
they shelter foreign dreams
for those who give love
without subtracting oblivion.

Shipwreck Among Olives

Permanence of a dazzling green
that pretends to be always relaxed
masking strength with restraint
so typical in the false surf
of the unmoving waters of the East.
Their tiny leaves rise in revolt
immortal they plough up the creases
of the last drop of sand.
Tempi nonexistent in the absence
of music, they revert to the silence
that weaves wreaths of olives.

Focus on the Languages of Africa

Translated by Georgina Collins

Only two of Mame Seck Mbacké's poems have been published in translation before, and yet her poetry is not only stylistically innovative but is rich with references to Senegalese history and culture, tackling issues of war, immigration, initiation rites and the African landscape, for example. Mame Seck Mbacké writes in both French and Wolof (a language of Senegal). Her work is incredibly varied – one of her poetry collections was written for the national football team, with a poem for each player. It is a far cry from the works of many first-wave Senegalese women writers who published poems not long after Senegalese independence in 1960. Many of these focused on redressing the gender balance by communicating the stories of women and creating more rounded and varied characters in literature, a necessary task. As part of the second wave of writers, Seck Mbacké has chosen a different route and the three poems here are just a small taste of a much larger body of work.

'Prayer on the Wing of Time' and 'Maro' both appear in a Francophone collection *Pluie-Poésie, Les Pieds sur la mer* (2000). Her poems in this collection appear as they do in the translations: one line runs into the next, the spaces indicating pauses in the poem, pauses that represent the way a tale may be performed to an audience as in oral tradition. 'Prayer on the Wing of Time' makes reference to Africa's history of slavery, colonisation and drought.

The title of the second poem, 'Maro', alludes to both thirst and fertility. In particular the title makes reference to the mythological Greek Priest Maro(n) who, as son or grandson of Dionysus, provided the wine that subdued the Cyclops Polyphemus (son of Poseidon and God of the sea). Mar also means 'thirst' in Wolof, which links us to the Djollof kingdom, that sat between the Ferlo desert and the Atlantic. There are of course many other connections we could make here, for instance, the poem could also be making reference to Virgil (Publius Vergilius Maro). The bovine goddess probably refers to the Egyptian goddess, Hathor (although there are others), who represents the sky, love and fertility.

Finally 'Waltz for the Harmattan' appears in the collection *Les Alizés de la souffrance* (2001). The Harmattan is a hot and dusty trade wind that blows in from the Sahara during the winter months. When it meets the cooler summer winds of the monsoon it has been known to create tornados, generating the historical, political and cultural chaos of the poem below.

Les Alizés de la souffrance, Poésie, Mama Seck Mbacké, © Éditions L'Harmattan (2001)
Prière sur l'aile du temps, Mama Seck Mbacké, © Éditions L'Harmattan (2001)

Prayer on the Wing of Time

I slept   Upon a water lily
So I could dream of fertile paddy fields
Of verdant fields   Of endless golden
harvests   Of beautiful flowering arteries
Of hanged gardens   And handsome
Youths   Marching with a confident stride

On the line of the horizon The opalescent
wedding of the water and the blue

Cease the sobbing for the Genocide
Cease the sorrow for the Drought   Let
laughter flow like waterfalls   To bring
together hearts   And warmth of spirit

MAMA SECK MBACKÉ

For Africa the Great   Land captured Now
serene

By the blissful sea   I returned to my lyre

And strengthen the strings

For an anthem of the   World

Maro

I love you so much That I turned my back   On
Worthless riches   So I could die from the quiver
your hands incite   Daybreak unfolds

Maro!

I want to walk with you   on the ochre land of
the Ferlo   Breathe the sweet silence of Djoloff
nights   From here to the stars Maro! I want to
milk the huge udder   Of the Bovine Goddess
With you   Grow drunk on the mystical milk
Maro   Become your eternal Eurydice   Beneath
the Samba rhythm dressed in a diaphanous robe

Maro!

To sleep   far   from   fictitious   constraints
When the night starts to sing   To live the
phantasmagoria of the flower of life   With my
rosary of nacreous laughter To open the prisons
of the soul   So the doves may fly

Maro!

To sing the hymn of newborns   On the green
horizon of sleeping marigolds   Never believing
for the sake of believing   Maro   To roar with
laughter   For the eternal idyll of our spirits

God of sand dunes son of water   In view of the
pasture   The sky kneels down before The
rainbow of our union   One thousand suns
sleeping with the smile of the Beloved!   Ten
thousand sighs upon the mouth of the Beloved!
My melodious flute your voice   Take my hand,
Maro! Guide me beyond the pathways of thorns

My foot the sea My head the sky   I carry the
boundless receptacle of nature   My secret
charm... Myself Maro!

Our laughter coalesced   Maro! Inexpressible
Beauty   And I leapt up to the skies   To dance
on the Morning Star

Without fear Maro!

I proclaimed my passion to the Gods   Without
fear Maro!   I will brave the age-old tempests
of your kind Without fear   my passage towards
the dulcet dawns

Maro!

And my plea   Banished damnations   And my
plea   Enlightened dungeons   The laughter

Maro!

And my plea   Sky with the odour of sanctity
The stars   bow down before   the   purity of my
Heart   Which sings of futures full of light

Waltz for the Harmattan

The Place Concorde
Discord of the People
Snow in heat
Nostalgia for the Africa
Of my nights
Of Samba Creole
Crooning
Along with Pigalle.
On Boulevard Barbès
The beggar goes *nyet, nyet, nyet*

On his shoulders
Red Square
Sheep drunk on vodka
Waltzing employers
Without contracts
In Montmartre
Palettes on strike
Drinking all the paint
From the Louvre
Vomits
Before Tutankhamun
Napoleon
Son of Leon the Neapolitan
The obelisk
On its back
Eats
The whole desert
With the pyramids
For dessert

RECAREDO SILEBO BOTURU AND
DAVID SHOOK

Writing in Bubi: a conversation

When I first met Recaredo Silebo Boturu in Malabo in 2011, his debut collection of poems had just been published in Spain. While on that trip to Equatorial Guinea I learned about his mother tongue, the Bubi language, and we had several discussions about its relationship to Spanish, especially within the literary landscape of Equatorial Guinea. The following poems, part of a book-length collection in progress, are what came from that conversation. Deeply grounded in Bubi culture and orality, these poems portray the imagery and voice of an island people, intimate with both the mountain and the sea.

The first moment I ever saw Boturu was after an hour-long interrogation by the police commissioner in a small room with blacked-out windows at the Malabo airport. He had come to pick me up, never having met me in person, and embraced me as if we had been lifelong friends. That embrace, in the kind of politically tense environment that would have inspired many of those familiar with the Obiang regime to flee entirely, epitomizes what is to me Boturu's greatest quality: he is relentlessly brave, both in his friendships as in his work to decry injustice, primarily by means of his work as a playwright, actor, and poet. The last poem of this bunch, a mere three lines of protest against his nation's infamously ruthless prison 'Black Beach', could easily be enough to land a Guinean writer in its confines. And yet Boturu continues to write and to publish, now in the Bubi language, confident in his belief that by doing so he makes the world a better place. I hope you will agree.

DAVID SHOOK: *How many languages do you speak? Which or which ones do you consider your mother tongue?*

RECAREDO SILEBO BOTURU: I speak Bubi [a language of Equatorial Guinea], French, Pichinglis, and Castilian. Bubi is my mother tongue.

DS: *Don't you speak Portuguese too?*

RSB: Eu falo.

DS: *When did you decide to start writing in Bubi and why?*

RSB: I decided to start writing in Bubi two years ago. When I realized that I as an individual could do something for my language. And I felt the need to do so. And that I had many things to tell and share.

DS: *What is the health of the language? Is it still spoken in the home? Is it used outside the context of the village? Has Bubi suffered from the use of the Fang language [from mainland Equatorial Guinea] by the majority of the politically powerful?*

RSB: The island of Bioko, our island, has always suffered under the colonization of other races, tongues, and cultures. And the Bubi people as a resulting idiosyncrasy have suffered the consequences of those colonizations. I must recognize that the Bubi language like other minority languages is in danger of extinction. There is not nor has there ever been any social or governmental structure to sustain the fecundity of our language and that accounts for the decline of our language in the home and in the village.

What did you learn when you began to write in Bubi? What differences do you find between the act and process of writing in Bubi versus writing in Spanish?

RSB: To write in Bubi is to reencounter my childhood and my ancestors. It connects me to the umbilical cord that connects me to my ancestors, to my land. Writing in Bubi is like discovering my weaknesses and strengths. My writing in Bubi depends greatly on my lexical and structural knowledge of Castilian. I learned Castilian in school because our national languages aren't taught. I recognize that my knowledge of my language is very circumscribed but when I face the challenge of writing I find my curiosity and courage grow.

DS: *What future do you imagine for your language?*

RSB: The future depends on what we do today. The state should take an active role in the struggle for the survival of our national languages because in the present day we can't expect much from the family structure given its brokenness. We should make a serious diagnosis and then act accordingly, abandoning partisan and tribalist idealogical struggles. One of the great stumbling blocks is that many have made us feel that we are small and we have bought the lie. We must believe and truly demonstrate that we are immense and grand.

DS: *What are some of the coolest things about your language? What makes it unique?*

RSB: Well, that question deserves an answer from Doctor [Justo] Bolekia, the great scholar and expert on our languages, but as a poet and playwright I'll tell you that my language has an impressive repetitive imagery, a historical reference to yesterday and a vision of tomorrow.

Is writing in Bubi a political act in and of itself?

I don't know. Writing in Bubi is a vital and spiritual necessity. It's a struggle to rediscover myself.

Does poetry exist in the Bubi tradition? What's it like? How has it influenced your work as a poet and playwright?

The Bubi poetry tradition is what would be known as 'song'. For us Bubis poetry-song is present in all that we do. From a creature's birth to when people cry at a burial, they cry in song, there's a lot of poetry in that act. There's poetry when we converse, when we perform traditional rituals, when we advise or seek advice. And I as a poet and playwright find it gratifying to utilize these attractive, potent images.

Translated by David Shook

We've Stumbled

The night disappeared,
the roosters crowed,
the dew drenched the men who left for the fields at dawn,
the sun came out
and the night's noise quieted.

We danced, we sang,
we ate, we got drunk!
We didn't do the traditional things
and the guardian spirits left in the lush forest.

The aubergine plant dried up,
and the women that went out fishing with their poles
and couldn't fish eels,
their bait rotted.
The sea was crying.

I'm Scared

I'm not afraid of the night's harmattan,
I'm not afraid of the dogs' howl,
I'm not afraid of the waves' shout,
I'm not afraid of the swamp that lies before my house,
I'm not afraid of the night,
I'm not afraid of midday storms.
I'm afraid of the forest's death,
of my mother's torment,
of the darkness of midday,
of the elderly stumbling,
of the anguish of the villages,
I am afraid of the death of my language,
I am afraid that the children's smiles be dispelled.
  Let's wake up!

Tocobe

She was an orphan
She climbed the slopes
Crossed the river
She was decimated by the sun's rays
And beaten by the rains
She was an orphan
She snaked her way to the village
She entered the hut and
Grandpa rang a bell over her head
The healer anointed her with ashes
And the holy red earth.
And the swamp dried up
And a path opened through it
And the line of ants disappeared

Black Beach

We have an abscess on our conscience,
a poison pumping through our veins.
Black Beach.

Translated by Lawrence Schimel

Born in Porto-Novo in Benin in 1960, Agnès Agboton has lived in
Barcelona since 1978. She is the author of many books on African
culture written in Spanish or Catalan, especially collections of oral
legends and traditions and cookbooks, but for her poetry Agnès
writes in her mother tongue, Gen, and then translates herself
into Spanish. She has published two bilingual poetry collections,
Canciones del poblado y el exilio (2006) and *Voz de las dos orillas* (2009).
The poems here are from *Canciones*.

 Agnès had been invited to represent her native Benin for the
Poetry Parnassus coinciding with the 2012 London Olympics, and
needed translations into English of her poems to read at the event.
Working through Spanish as the bridge language (she had been
unable to find any direct translators between Gen and English), I
translated a selection of poems from her two collections. Since Gen
is a tonal language, translating the musicality of her work was as
important as the meaning. During many long phone conversations,
Agnès read the original versions of her poems to me, so I could hear
the sound, and I in turn read aloud the English versions, which we
revised, tweaking word choice and word order until we had a final
draft which sounded right. I'm pleased that these translations will
now reach a readership beyond those fortunate enough to have been
able to attend the Poetry Parnassus and hear them read aloud.

1.

Here, where time
seems to have stopped.
Here, where the land
is abandoned,
sacrificed daily
to useless memories
and heroic songs.
Here, where blood
seems fruitless.
Here, in the stillness
of the cemetery,
I've still found
the steady gaze
of crushed eyes,
I've listened to the words
of a stiffened tongue.
I've glimpsed life.

3.

My eyes seek nudes
in the land of masks,
where even smiles
                    disguise themselves.
Are there traces of foreign clothes

on your naked body?
Do your hands also, sometimes,

                        disguise themselves?

Your eyes on the swing
shift from smiles to weeping.

They smile full of tears,
they cry among guffaws
and there's always a slight
fissure
for fright.

Your eyes on the swing
shift from smiles to weeping;
they move from weeping to smiles
and open themselves to fright.

Your eyes on the swing.
Black flowers,
laughter and lament.

22.

It seems
that in your eyes you have
two needles.

Two small needles
in a black sea;
tell me, you who gaze at me,
whether I too have them.

Sometimes
your needles
bite my flesh.

They dance upon the pillow
almost drowned
when the sea of your eyes
has overflowed.

30.

Through their veins flows
night and morning
and in all their gestures
the dance is born.

I counted, one by one, their fingers
now far away,
I approach its skin of foam
and I saw that look
ignite in their eyes.

The dance is born, yes,
the dance is born.

AGNÈS AGBOTON

I then saw how, in them,
two continents sprouted.
Their steps were white,
all their complaints were black,
those words.

The dance is born, yes,
the dance is born.

I now take refuge in their arms,
the new shoots,
with the sun at one extreme
and dark scent in these leaves,
I curl around.

The dance is born, yes,
the dance is born.

Who will stop those rivers?
Who will channel that wind?

It is already an enormous flow
that lifts those bodies,
through all their veins flow
the nights and the mornings.

And they are a dance, yes,
they are a dance.

Green and Brown

I asked my friend the translator, What was the first known act of
translation in the history of mankind? His answer was, Probably
something into or out of Egyptian. I thought about this for a while
and ventured a certainty: No, I said, it was when a mother heard her
baby babble or cry, and had to decide an instant what it meant.

– 'Short Lecture On Translation' from *Twenty-Two Short Lectures*
– Mary Ruefle

I found the 'Short Lecture...' above on Twitter and instantly saved a
copy, because it rang true, because it is sublimely written, because it
echoed things I'd said about poetry: the first poem happened when a
cavegirl tried describing the sunrise to her caveguy. She was reaching
towards the poetic: after internalising the world, she was attempting
to capture and externalise her point of view, communicate its
personal significance entirely in words.

I was born to a Muslim father and a Christian mother who hailed
from different tribes in Nigeria and spoke different languages: my
father Uwano and Hausa, my mother Isoko and Yoruba. Their only
common tongue was English and this was the language spoken
to and around me. English then is my mother tongue but not my
mother's and I imagine, when she tried to understand my babble, she
articulated it to herself first in Isoko, then translated her responses
to herself in English, before whispering them to the babbling me.

I wonder what happened in the seconds or milliseconds between her decoding of my language and her English kicking in. I wonder what instinctive utterances were lost, what soothings she grew up on that I never got.

◆

A friend, the author and publisher Nii Ayikwei Parkes, described visiting his ancestral village in Ghana after spending years in the capital. There, he said, his mother tongue is used for basic day-to-day communication requesting typical things. However, returning to the village, to its context, to the very grounds on which the language stewed, he realised the deep connection it had to the flora and fauna, that the words and environment cross-referenced each other; the green seemed greener somehow, the browns browner... There were cultures and colours locked inside the language.

◆

The Kenyan writer Ngugi Wa Thiong'o asserts that language is of vital importance to culture and when African writers write in English, they expand and deepen the metaphysical (English) empire at the expense of their own languages and cultures. He had found this so problematic that despite his awards and legions of English-reading fans across the world, he turned away from writing in it and reverted to his mother tongue of Gikuyu. He writes in this tongue first, deepening, I imagine, his connection to himself, his ancestry, his fatherland.

◆

Last year I began working on *The Calm*, a play and prequel to
Shakespeare's *The Tempest* for the Royal Shakespeare Company.
In preparation, I read and re-read *The Tempest* and each reading
revealed it to be an unsettling play. At turns it is comedic, yet there
is a tragic longing haunting it. Though the characters are Italian,
they feel authentically British. There's a young, fantastic love story
at its heart, yet the central conflict is around old men and power. It
praises the pursuit and gathering of knowledge, yet discards all at
the close of the play. Most problematic for me was its treatment of
Caliban, who begins the play a slave and though there is forgiveness
and everyone else lives happily ever after, Caliban ends the play a
slave. Much has been written about Caliban's dialect, how Prospero
gifted him language, which not only did he bastardise by peppering
it with the flora and fauna of the island, but used it to curse Prospero
relentlessly. However, within the world of the play, Caliban must
have had and spoken a language before Prospero's colonisation.
Sycorax would have spoken to him in this tongue, would have
translated his babble into this, responded quickly in it, and Caliban
would have had a stronger connection to himself, his ancestry, his
fatherland. I think his bastardising of Prospero's tongue was a way of
stamping his authority on it, of carrying over aspects of his culture,
of making greens greener and the browns browner.

Elias Canetti wrote 'The inklings of poets are the forgotten
adventures of God.' Taking Shakespeare as a god of the world
of *The Tempest*, and myself as the poet armed with inclination, I
wonder what Ariel, a native spirit of the island, and Caliban might
have spoken about. Both would know the local language – what
words might they have had for 'Tempest' or 'Calm'? What concepts

might've been untranslatable? What secrets of the island did Prospero never know? What would have been impossible for him to understand? What might have been Island poems and psalms?

◆

In Kenya, Sheng is some way related to Caliban's tongue. A mixture of the official languages of Swahili and English, it further draws from dialects in its immediate vicinity. In contemporary Nigeria where my play is set, an equivalent to Sheng is Nigerian Pidgin English, which breaks down and mixes English with local languages. Pidgin, spoken by over 50 million Nigerians, is the lingua franca of the country. It was popularised by the lower and working classes and my Caliban figure, domestic servant Jennifer, who is of this class, speaks entirely in this language.

◆

Caliban:
Be not afeard; the isle is full of noises,
Sounds and sweet airs, that give delight and hurt not.
Sometimes a thousand twangling instruments
Will hum about mine ears, and sometime voices
That, if I then had waked after long sleep,
Will make me sleep again: and then, in dreaming,
The clouds methought would open and show riches
Ready to drop upon me that, when I waked,
I cried to dream again.

◆

Jennifer:
Mek you no fear; de kitchen get plenty noise
but e dey sweet me, e go relax you, no shaking.
Sometimes na pot and pan go dey play together,
dey rub my ear, sometimes na person voice...
and even if long sleep just commot for my eye,
e go make me wan sleep again. I go dream
sey clouds go open and money wey dey there,
go shower me, and even wen I wake pata pata,
I jus wan dream again.

◆

The governing attempt in my play, is to transpose or translate
aspects of *The Tempest* for a contemporary theatre audience, to, in
the setting of modern day Nigeria, make the greens greener and
browns browner.

Translated by Charles Cantalupo

Reesom Haile (1946–2003) believed that his country, Eritrea, was best
known through its languages – in his case, Tigrinya – and specifically
through Eritrea's literature. From the first moment I heard him
performing his poetry at the Expo cultural festival in Asmara to
an audience of thousands in August 1998, I knew he was right. I've
known it ever since. But all too often Eritrea is discussed, like many
African nations, as if it has no literature: as if, especially for readers
of poetry, Eritrea has no poetry that reveals 'the best that has been
thought and said' about Eritrea, as is the case, especially for readers
of poetry, in all nations. For two decades, therefore, the recognition
of the power of Eritrean literature, particularly its poetry, has been
my passion, as my new book, *Where War Was – Poems and Translations
of Poems from Eritrea* (Mkuki na Nyota, 2016), confirms, yet as the
following translations reinforce. To know Eritrea is to read – to
witness – the poetry Reesom Haile wrote in Tigrinya over five years
like one long *annus mirabilis*. For example, he published 'Teshewano'
or 'To My Graceful People' in 1996, 1998, and 2002, yet the internal
and intense Eritrean politics it highlights – 'We can cultivate the art
to unite, | Or fight each other and fall apart' – could be as much an
issue now, as Eritrea celebrates its Silver Jubilee, as when the nation
was in its romantic infancy. Reesom emailed 'Shakespeare, Enough'
to me in February 2002, roughly a year after 'Teshewano' – a year
in which he emailed me hundreds of poems, new poems, several a
day sometimes, for possible inclusion in our forthcoming second
collection, *We Invented the Wheel*. He often wrote a gloss for any poem
he sent, but all he said about this one is 'Shakespear did it. A little
conceit.' England; Eritrea. I say it again. What nation can be known,
without its literature being known? Still, the literature of Eritrea, like
the poetry of Reesom Haile, is all too often unheard.

To My Graceful People

Dear hunters, and you at the hearth,
You gatherers, and you in the house,

In your camo to fight,
In your *netselas*, travelling light,
In your workout or business suits,
In your sandals, sneakers, or boots –

We can cultivate the art to unite,
Or fight each other and fall apart.

Why hate? Why separate?
We all decide our country's fate.

Enough with the opposites:
Sinner or saint, blessing or curse –
They only make our problems worse.

To please or displease, praise or condemn,
Frighten or fear, adore or dismiss –
We've been in this abyss.
Together we break out.

Enough polarizing
Who lives or dies?
End it. Let peace rise.

Note: *Netselas* are traditional cloaks

REESOM HAILE

Shakespeare, Enough

Shakespeare said,
Aren't my poems great?
How about that love story
Of Romeo and Juliet?

But I replied,
Shakespeare, enough.
Who wants old stuff
Like that?

Why not
A new kind of love?
A love of Eritreans
For green Eritrea,

Not yet found in words,
Unheard –
A fearless story
The angels sing.

Writing my poems,
Living as long
As Methusaleh,
I couldn't end this song
Before God called me home.

Translated by Chege Githiora

Gĩkũyũ (Kikuyu) is one of the many languages of Kenya. It has a significant body of published literature, among them the longest novel in an African language written by Ngũgĩ wa Thiong'o, and translated by himself as *The Wizard of the Crow*. But not much more Gĩkũyũ literature has been translated into western languages. This is the first time, and with his collaboration, that Gĩtahi's poetry (*marebeta*) can be enjoyed in English. Reflecting on life, society, culture and politics, he voices the thoughts of many at home in Africa, and in the Diaspora. In one of the translated poems, 'Where I was born' he vividly captures nostalgia and the yearning for 'home'. Gĩtahi is ever preoccupied with the importance of preserving African languages by writing in them, and teaching them to African children. Yet Gĩtahi is not just longing for a lost past, his masterly use of language through deployment of metaphor, word play and humour links his work to traditional oral artistry of the Gĩkũyũ people, such as the dialogic poetry form known as *Gĩcandĩ*. His poetry and short stories are laden with humour, imagery, metaphor and linguistic innovations which all serve to enrich the Gĩkũyũ language's literary bank. A note on the translation of the poem 'Chief Crocodile' is necessary. Chiefs in Kenya were created to enforce colonial rule and exploitation at the grassroots, for example, by forcibly recruiting labour to work on European farms. They wielded brutal power in a manner befitting the values of the system that created them, thus they became a focus of resentment by the colonised population. The chiefs' roles did not change much in the post-colony, and they continue to be regarded by some as agents of oppressive authority and corruption.

Where I was Born

Yesterday was fine, just weaver birds quarrelling
sated with pecking on fresh maize growing in the fields
the red eye of the sun shone hard at me
and the clouds frowned
the mist shrouding the mountains
like so much cloth

children mock the sobbing wood doves
the voices of people on their way
to and from the market
are like a voice lost
in the thunder's underclothes

the roofs and eaves of houses
are like smoking mushrooms
the cries of calves and lambs
are taken up by their mothers
the clang of pots and milk pails
as tithe is demanded of the cows

you hear the *ko-ko-ko!*
of axes and hammers
as houses and fences are mended
of wood being split
for poles and firewood

a lorry moans up the hill
like one about to give birth
laden with sacks of produce
on its way to the city
to feed its dwellers

when rain-clouds gather
farmers tut
at losing time to work the land
when so much time is needed

as livestock return to the kraal
children are kept out of the way
lightning strikes like swords of fire
while lovers seek each other in corners
so they too can rain, as the rain falls
the cold needs banishing

I saw this with my own eyes
From my vantage point
while on a quiet stroll
to where I shall not reveal
no matter what you do

GĨTAHĨ GĨTĨTĨ

Chief Crocodile

What is a chief like?
a chief is like a crocodile
let loose in a market
mouth watering for others' goods

chief in his khaki
chief with his guards
chief with his greed
his belly large
like a yawning chasm

chief is like a wild dog
who eats the lion's leftovers
or like a vulture who
cannot tell the difference
between a meat feast
and the meat of a dead dog
run over by a car.

Translated by Cheryl Moskowitz

Seyoum's writing combines the sharp and satirical with the tender and moving, and often wrestles with conflicting ideologies in Ethiopian identity. Seyoum says of these two poems: 'The title 'Portrait of the Beggar as an Old Woman' is an allusion to James Joyce. The poem is part of my attempt to paint the lives of poor folk in a fast-growing city. 'Trying to Forget You' is about the attempt to forget the one you love. The wonder of nature that springs from *Kiremt* (the rainy season in Ethiopia) might serve as a distraction but ultimately the struggle to forget is ironically another way of remembering.'

Portrait of the Beggar as an Old Woman

By a busy road in Addis
under a brand new building
the old beggar woman rests,
curled on the ground like a bracelet made of grass.
She has pulled a belt tight around her middle
as if she fears Hunger
might suddenly leap like a mad beast from her belly
and bite the passers by.

Though the Universe can decorate the wings of a butterfly
and paint the leaves of an oak tree,
it has covered this woman in dirt from head to toe.
The building that towers above her is a monster
with glass eyes and a brick body.
The woman is his trophy.

Trying to Forget You

The rain is walking on the ceiling of my house
The bedroom curtain is waving like a white flag
The oak leaves are cupping rainwater from the sky
to wet the dry throat of the earth
The earth is imbibing new life
Next to all this natural grace, your leaving is nothing
I am trying to forget you
The rain's footsteps come close, closer
Kiremt messiah of all new creatures, has shown up right on time
A dense fog has veiled your beautiful face
The smell of wet soil has taken the place of your perfume
I am trying to forget you
The rain stamps its feet violently
The sky we shared falls like the bark of an old oak
A new sky is born
A river is born
The river washes away your footprint, and the road you walked away on
I am trying to forget you

Translated by Fasika Ayelew and Chris Beckett

Bedilu Wakjira is a new discovery for me. He is a professor at Addis
Ababa University and a prolific journalist and poet. I found his three
Amharic poetry collections on a crowded bookstall in Piassa and
started to read them in my hotel. But I needed help and was lucky
enough to be contacted by Fasika Ayalew, a poet who came across
my article on Ethiopian poetry in *The Missing Slate* in March. Fasika
chose a few of Bedilu's poems which she liked and sent me her own
poetic translations, rather than literals. We then went back and forth
between the original text and Fasika's translations, looking for ways
to convey the distinctive personality of Bedilu's extended metaphors,
his frequent repetitions and informal but elegant syntax; and, of
course, to serve the important message of hope which shines out of
every Bedilu poem and is what makes him such an inspiring writer.

If People Were Rocks

If people were rocks, or marble
you could carve into lovely shapes,
work their rough edges, chips
and snags, bring out the individual –
I'd place them slowly in a pile
and build my country like a dry stone wall.
If people were rocks, I'd like to be a mason.

Longing for Spring

Our country, our times: you overwhelm us!
But still hope grows in us
like a rose, a bud of the good in us,
even if it does not flower
or wither...
a leaf is enough, if the roots go deep!
hope is enough, if the bud breathes deep!

We can dig it up, throw it away
but hope is such a part of us, it will not go away.
Time teases us, steals our bloom
but still we long for something good to bloom.
For children of an unlit dawn, always living on hope –
tell us, what else is there to do?

*(scribbled with troubled feelings in May 1989 when 'a few'
generals tried to stage a coup against the Derg military
government)*

What You Say to Me

Don't come! is what you say to me
when you're struggling with your soul
and beating yourself up

you are the pain in me! is what you say to me
and tuck yourself away in a retreat
and treat me like a sin

I'm locking my front door! is what you say to me
switching off your lamp

don't come! is what you say to me
but then you sit there
and I know you're waiting just for me

Translated by Alemu Tebeje and Chris Beckett

Zewdu is a wonderfully modest poet and professor who lives in
Gondar, the beautiful old northern capital of Ethiopia. When I
met him there this February he wanted to explain every word and
phrase of every poem we discussed! He is passionately critical of
himself and Ethiopians generally for being so politically docile. He
brought many pages of hand-written notes to the hotel where we had
breakfast looking out over the city. His poems are often allegorical,
with layers of meaning you can only unlock if you appreciate
Ethiopia's contemporary political context. I used Zewdu's notes
(even copying some of his phrases) to help me get to the quick of his
poems. My translations are not always close to the Amharic words
in Zewdu's poems, but I hope they convey his very engaging style
and the serious import of what he is saying. I am grateful to Alemu
Tebeje for his collaborative help with these translations.

The Fashion of Silence

Our academic beards
grew long and thick,
we never combed our hair.
'I don't need much!'
we'd say, our trousers
thin as hermits
under our itchy coats.
We discussed
everything that mattered
in the world, tearing
our opinions out like pages
from a breathing book.

But that's all gone:
our hair is slapped with oil
and smartly trimmed,
our leaner bodies
own a rack of shiny epithets,
our shirts and ties
are mute, even our jackets
don a pensive look
but oh! our baggy pants
are loose enough
to hide a thousand secrets
and whisper when we walk.

The temper of the times
has changed, we do not dare
discuss a thing of
all those everythings
that mattered
and still matter in the world –
today our House of Learning
wears a fashionable hush.

Your Smile

Show me your lovely teeth!
don't spoil it by eating or drinking,
don't say a word or turn your head –
I just want to watch your teeth
shining like a row of pearls.
My eyes shine too when I see you smile!
My heart blunders off the path
but my eyes are true and they forgive me.

Our Journey

It was a long wide road
and we set off together,
just you and me,
walking up that long wide road
wider than a country,
long as modern history.

After many days and months
and a full bucket of years,
you said, 'why don't we stop?'
and the place you said this
looked a lot like
where we'd set off from.

Cooked and Raw

Something cooked and something raw,
when mixed together, go to war.
But that's not all, as cooked cooks more,
it burns, so it might as well be raw.

When Ethiopians cook together,
however fast we stir,
our kind perceptive people burn
before the gullible learn.

Translated by Stephen Walsh

These two deceptively simple and accessible poems are typical of
the work of the Zimbabwean novelist and poet Ndabezinhle Sigogo
(1932–2008). Sigogo wrote in siNdebele, the language of the minority
ethnic group who live in the south-east of the country. The poems,
like much of Sigogo's work, are rooted in the landscape, culture and
structures of rural life in Matabeleland.

The Bride Leaves Home

The road that people's much-loved children take
When, bags upon their backs, they leave their homes
To live like foreigners in strangers' houses,
Is actually that same mysterious route
God made the day He made Adam and Eve
To show him where to find forbidden fruit.

For when they pour their blessings on your head,
And call upon your ancestors to come
And be with you, it is because to wed
Can be to walk barefoot on thorns. Of course
Sometimes it is a primrose path – some brides
Forget their homes and grow as fat as beasts.

But, lovely one, when you must leave your kin,
And old folk gather, and you want to scorn
The words of god-like wisdom they pass on –
Those words will come to pierce you like a dart,

Those words will later sound your inner thoughts,
Make you forget what's held in your own heart.

And when we sing, *Look after her, please,*
Look after her, our father's orphan child,
On our behalf – who wrote that song of praise?
We know it comes from deep inside our souls –
And women cry as if they mourn a death,
For marriage is a funeral to them.

And you, the bride, the one who is to wed –
You need to steel yourself, make yourself strong.
Forget your father's house, its welcome breadth,
The high mountains of home. Leave them behind
And come into your new home on your knees –
On your knees or belly to the ground.

The day you'll wed is that same day you'll see
That humans can transform themselves to beasts.
So hitch your warm heart safely to a tree
With a long rope you've taken there with you,
And keeping your own ear tightly to the ground
For news, say nothing. Don't make a sound.

Will You Come With Me...?

My love, will you come with me
to those far-off mountains
you can climb till you grow old?
There are rivers to cross, up,
high up, where the bees die off –
but my bags are all packed,

my love. Will you come with me
as far as those mountains?
Not everyone can get there –
for there is always another peak
over the ridge, wooded, green
with scores of beasts that lie in wait,

my love. Will you come with me
as I face the darkest woods?
As I brave the fog that shrouds
the monsters and the lions?
Will you be with me, my love,
as I walk among the ruins?

My love, will you come with me
if I make towards the east?
Will you come west with me,
or if our path turns north?
Even a footstep on a python's tail
is part of our destined journey.

My love: will you stay with me
even if my muscles cramp?
Even if my legs go lame,
or the gorges make me blind?
And when the hornets buzz
all of life's hope out of me,

my love, will you come with me
to the plains? Will you
come with me through the trees?
In the light, and through the night,
and even in the thickest forests
in the hardest of times?

And even if I sink in the slough –
then let us sink together. My love.

Translated by Michele Hutchison

For a while now I have been translating Alfred Schaffer's latest collection *Mens dier ding* [Human Animal Thing, 2014]. Partly inspired by *Chaka*, a famous South African novel from 1931 written by Thomas Mofolo, the book charts the imaginary progress of the nineteenth-century statesman and tyrant, Shaka Zulu (1787–1828). Structured around a series of daydreams and major events in Zulu's life, the poet extracts Zulu from the historical past and moves him to the modern media age where speed dating, UFOs and effervescent painkillers are the norm. The collection is hugely diverse and eclectic, from lyrical poetry to tweets. Schaffer identifies strongly with his subject and the two begin to merge in a fascinating manner, as do the personal and the historical, resulting in a unique and highly original collection.

A black man armed with a spear caused a commotion during yesterday's evening rush hour by prostrating himself across the motorway which happened to run through the man's place of abode.

Drivers struggled to avoid the man.
The man was under the influence, according to police.
But what does that mean, 'under the influence'.
A good question, actually, it's such a broad concept.
Under the influence, he appeared aggressive and confused.
It took some real effort to finally apprehend the man.
The police had to resort to physical violence to handcuff him.
It's hard to imagine that he is still alive so let us pray.

Hard facts about shaka, in other words hard facts about me

Because the facts have to be laid on the table.
Name: Shaka. S-H-A-K-A. Exactly as you say it.
First fact. I'm based on all kinds of things
but not on the truth – *yeah kiddo, you'd love that, wouldn't you?*
my mother used to say.

What a coincidence that I was born in Africa!
Africa is big and dry, sometimes it rains in Africa
is Africa a country, I don't think so.
Who knows, Africa may be the orphan of the world economy.
The first man learned to hop and skip here but
what does the 8,512,784,325,236,108,946,347th person know about Africa?

I'm a blank screen, a black warrior
with ebony skin and a transparent soul.
I'm posing as Napoleon for my Facebook profile pic
my left foot rests on a servant's head.

I raised and saved a nation of people.
My father was called He Who Has Good Reasons For What He Does.
A man never takes the floor in his father's presence
except when his father asks him something.
I'm not much of a family man, my birth
was a scandal, dry humping that got out of hand.

'Look, a UFO.' My first words.
According to rumours, I was conceived during Mardi Gras.
Other rumours say that I was begotten in a river.
The best version, I think, is the one about the night-time car park
in the heart of the tundra.

I use Makassaroil™ to cover the grey hairs.
Good stuff, not sticky and it doesn't stain.
According to sources, I'm 6 foot 4", according to others
I've got a hunchback and a speech defect.
Usain Bolt, Jesse Owens: mediocre runners.
According to eyewitnesses I bludgeoned a leopard
to pulp as a young teen.
According to others, I was teased about my tiny cock.

An entire herd of water buffalo was used
to film the slaughter of a single buffalo in *Apocalypse Now*.

I know more than a hundred names for 'water buffalo'.
I only know one for 'woman'.

The short-handed stabbing spear, that's my invention.
'The *assegaai*'s blade was longer than that of a regular spear –
    45 centimetres long and almost 4
centimetres wide – it was attached to a strong, short shaft. Shaka
    called this spear *iklwa*, after the
sucking noise it made when it was pulled out of a body after having
    been thrust in it
deeply.' End of quote.

How many facts is that so far? Just a few more then
everything that exists around us will be hand-made.
Mountains, snakes and rivers, everything inanimate and animate.
Everything outside of my territory is one big wasteland:
if [x] has to be killed then [x] will be killed
because [x] has nowhere to go.
When I see the vultures circling high above my head
I think Look at that, the king's birds are hungry!
And so I feed them.

I came on a boat from Africa to tell my story
a small boat carrying lots of people.
The odd person fell overboard along the way
it gave some relief but never for long.
Although we sailed on the open seas, it stank of cheese
and shit and alcohol on the boat
I also lost my favourite spear there.

I'm the legitimate heir of The Tramp, aka
Him With The Problems.
My favourite kit: a t-shirt and jeans
during the week, a turban and animal skin
on formal occasions.

Betray me and you betray my people.
Leading a nation of people is like pruning a garden.
The more you prune
the stronger the tree, the fuller the shrub.

An army is a starving monster, you have to keep feeding it.
My people had no idea.
On the battlefield there was some shouting back and forth
and a bit of rolling around, an idiotic chaos.
OK, *cut!* I shouted, this is just silly.
From that day onwards blood began to flow.

When everything was pretty much conquered, on the even days
death and I played eenie meenie miney mo.
I categorically refused door-to-door advertising.
When I wanted water I shouted Sister, water please!
I stopped reading the papers but I still watched sport and MTV
and I still kept a diary.

Fact: Martin Scorsese filmed almost every scene in *Raging Bull*
in black and white because of all the blood.
Yet the boxing scene in the film only lasts for 10 minutes.

I hear you ask But how does it work in practice.
With all those henchmen all that overtime?
Well, they work fast
a) break neck b) bash in skull c) impale the shit.
A head deeply impaled on a spike, now there
you have something resembling orgasm's famous face.

A leader without followers is a ghost
a ghost is like a restless spirit.
And what it's like death death death is pure television
complete bullshit, the script is crap
don't believe death death death.

'People who were found guilty of sorcery were impaled through the anus
        using a series of short,
pointed stakes until the neck was reached; after that they were
        abandoned to die in the veldt, prey
to vultures and hyenas.'
End of quote.

For a promotional film I stood in a vat filled with ice
for almost three hours, all kinds of stuff went wrong, the lights went out
the catering went on strike, the director got drunk.
I had just one line but what a line it was.
While in operettas all of the text has to be sung!

Each day I feel like I've drunk five bottles of wine
I float like vermicelli in a big pan of soup.
The soup is lukewarm with a layer of fat on top.

When I have guests, I pretend to be deaf.
'Just you see – when he's had his coffee
he'll start banging on about the war again.'

I still haven't settled on my final words.
What's going on, children of my fatherland? (Too weak.)
Are you killing me, king of the earth? (Too friendly.)
Let me be your servant! (Has already been said once.)
When I die this country will be occupied from all sides
by the shrewd white man, then we'll see something
mark my words! (Not sure I can remember all of that.)

What do I see when I look in the mirror? An undulating reflection
of a reflection of a reflection.
I call this the Droste effect
you call it Symbolism.

Last fact.
I am not dead.
Try and prove it.

Fathers and Children

Kirill Medvedev, *It's No Good*, edited and introduced by Keith
Gessen, translated by Keith Gessen with Mark Krotov, Cory Merrill
and Bela Shayevich, Ugly Duckling Presse, 2016

The broad features of Russian poetry during the post-Soviet period
were already in the process of formation during the last decade of
Soviet power. This was the era of 'janitors and watchmen', in which
many young writers, alienated from the world of official Soviet
culture, chose to support themselves by taking menial jobs, while
continuing to write and to disseminate their poems through an
unofficial literary culture based on samizdat and informal readings.

The poetry produced within this late Soviet alternative culture
tended to privilege purely literary values over social criticism.
Already convinced of the futility of committed literature by the
failure of the previous generation who had come of age during
Khrushchev's 'Thaw', these young poets were further encouraged
to cultivate a hermetic, highly literary poetry, oriented toward
difficulty and self-conscious sophistication, by the sealed-off
character of an unofficial literary scene in which they were deprived
of the possibility of a wider audience. The refusal of politics was, of
course, in itself a political act, given the Soviet regime's disapproval
of pure aestheticism in literature. But apart from this limited,
negative gesture, the poets of the underground were generally
reluctant to engage directly with social and political issues.

With the arrival of perestroika in the late 80s it was perhaps
inevitable that it should be the leading poets of the Soviet
counterculture who, having preserved their artistic integrity by
refusing to compromise with the ideological demands of Soviet
officialdom, went on to dominate the post-Soviet period with their

ideal of a pure poetry, untainted by politics. However in recent years these values have been increasingly called into question by a group of younger writers for whom the Olympian detachment of the literary establishment no longer seems viable amid the injustice, corruption and degradation of contemporary Russia.

One of the best known, and most interesting, of these rebellious younger poets is Kirill Medvedev, who was born in 1975 and lives and works in Moscow, a city which provides the backdrop to many of his poems. Medvedev's poetry is shaped by his refusal of the dominant poetics of the first decade of the post-Soviet era.

Again and again his poems declare, loudly and unceremoniously, their disdain for what the speaker of 'just a little more about literature:' – a poem which recounts the career of the Soviet poet Nikolay Rubtsov, translated here by Cory Merrill and Keith Gessen – contemptuously refers to as 'formalist tricks':

with rubtsov it wasn't so simple
at some point he lived in petersburg
where he spent time with the petersburg aesthetes
and trained himself in various formalist
tricks
he admired brodsky
and so on

In place of the classical metres and rhymes schemes of his predecessors, Medvedev offers us a rough free verse modelled on that of Charles Bukowski; and in place of their refined formal experimentation, Medvedev offers us seemingly shapeless, rambling anecdotes and meditations, gathered from the streets of contemporary Moscow. And to this is added an interest in the Russian tradition of civic verse which is reminiscent of the political turn of contemporary American poets such as Charles Bernstein.

And yet Medvedev's stance toward his elders is in fact rather more complex than one of unequivocal rejection, and he owes much to the example of the Moscow Conceptualist Dmitry Prigov. In an obituary of Prigov, included in this volume, Medevedev describes him as one of the great Russian poets of the post-war period, who must nonetheless be 'pushed away and overcome', and his poetry shares with Prigov's a pervasive sense of the absurdity of Russian reality. There is indeed a great deal more 'literature' in this writing than is at first apparent. What Medvedev offers his readers is rather an artfully constructed image of artlessness. His narratives and meditations, however many times they seem to be on the point of losing themselves in a maze of aimless digressions, somehow always win their way through to a coherent conclusion; and his apparently formless free verse is actually carefully crafted through his favourite devices of repetition, parallelism and suggestive rhythmic shifts between longer and shorter lines, the latter often consisting of a single heightened word. Above all, Medvedev's lyrical hero, with his meandering anecdotes and analyses of contemporary Russian life, opinionated yet self-doubting, as ready to contradict himself as to pass judgement on others, is an engaging literary creation with antecedents in the nineteenth-century classical novel. In the lyrical heroes of Kirill Medvedev, the children of contemporary Russia are once more in revolt against their fathers.

From the foregoing it will be apparent that that the task of translating Medvedev's poetry involves more than just transcribing its content, without regard for formal questions. The versions offered here are for the most part competent, though they do sometimes smooth out the cultivated roughness of Medvedev's Russian. The translations also have a tendency to follow the line-breaks of the original Russian a little mechanically, and as a result some of its more subtle rhythms and intonations can fall by the wayside and the resulting English seem a little flat. But perhaps for the same reason, the more emotionally heightened passages, for which Medvedev reserves his favourite 'formal tricks', negotiate the transition to English more successfully, as in the following extract from 'these are just small poems and nothing else', translated by Bela Shayevich, in which the poet-hero defends himself against the charge of stagnation:

and I told him, yes, I'd noticed that, too
I see what you're saying and, you know, I am already searching for
    (*already* searching for!)
some new *approaches*, subjects, *intonations*,
so it'll soon be different, soon
everything will be good again, just be patient a little more, please
a little more
a little more
(of the
same)

As Keith Gessen points out in his introduction, the plain style can often be the hardest to convey in English, a case in point being Medvedev's free verse, which though merely conventional in English, can be still be felt as daringly unorthodox in Russian. But overall, this generous selection of Kirill Medvedev's poems, essays and actions can be welcomed as a valuable addition to the corpus of contemporary Russian poetry in translation. Medvedev is one of the more interesting poets writing in Russian today, and we should be grateful to the consistently adventurous Ugly Duckling Presse for offering us this intriguing glimpse into an alternative poetic universe.

Stephen Capus

A Small Hall of Mirrors

12 *Greek Poems After Cavafy*, edited by Paschalis Nikolaou, translated by Paschalis Nikolaou & Richard Berengarten, Shearsman, 2015

For centuries translations have often become entwined with the text they transform so that, regardless of any issues of fidelity (or sometimes even quality), they have come to stand for their original. Renaissance Anglophone readers perceived Arthur Golding's *Metamorphoses* as the equivalent of Ovid's Latin epic. A few centuries later, rightly or wrongly, a generation of Victorian readers took Edward FitzGerald's colonialist deconstruction of Omar Khayyám's Persian quatrains as their own *Rubáiyát*. And in more recent times, since their publication in 1975, Edmund Keeley and Philip Sherrard's acclaimed and hugely popular versions of Alexandrian Greek poet C.P. Cavafy are now read – and quoted – as if they are the original.

Cavafy is a natural candidate for this sense of universal ownership. His demotic speech and inclusive dramatic monologues – captured so adroitly by Keeley and Sherrard – make us feel as if we know him, lulling us, like so many of his poems' protagonists, into a false sense of security. Yet Keeley and Sherrard's loose English verse often strays from Cavafy's own, more structured metrics. And so for Greek readers, and especially for Greek poets, there are many other Cavafys. Paschalis Nikolaou's exquisite new chapbook for Shearsman offers a glimpse of these often shadowy doppelgangers. It collects together twelve versions of and responses to the Alexandrian poet, presented both in their original Greek and in excellent facing English translations by Nikolaou and Richard Berengarten. Here is an impressive piece of editorial selection; as Nikolaou points out in his brief but fascinating introduction (additional material can be found online at www.shearsman.com), Greece has already seen two vast anthologies of Cavafy-inspired verse, both edited by Dimitris Daskalopoulos, and collectively containing a whopping 358 poems.

Nikolaou's more modest volume still manages to span a century of Greek poetry. It begins in 1916 with 'Alexander of Macedon', by Timos Malanos, who knew Cavafy personally, and ends in the present day with Dimitris Kosmopoulos's previously unpublished yet hugely affecting '16 March 2015, 6 p.m.'. In between there are familiar names such as Yannis Ritsos and George Seferis alongside those who might be less known but no less engaging. Zisis Oikonomou's 'At Chandragupta's Palace, 305 B.C.', for instance, conjures up a Cafavyesque clash between Hellenistic and Maryan culture through the voice of an enslaved Greek:

> we're two broken bodies
> tossed among piles of merchandise, abandoned
> to remembering emptiness

Meanwhile Northern Cypriot Kyriakos Charalambides's 'Three Horses, Olympic Prizewinners', echoes Cavafy's early poem 'The Souls of Old Men' with an equally beguiling melancholy:

> They no
> longer need to entangle manes or bridles
> with the perilous long hair of the temptress.

The deft imitations of Oikonomou and Charalambides are joined here by delicate evocations of the poet himself from Yorgos Sarandaris ('C.P.Cavafy') and Yannis Ritsos ('The Poet's Space') who imagines Cavafy in his Alexandria apartment:

wavering entire like a scale in the hand of god,
between the yes and the no, desire and regret,
while the light from the window behind him
rests on his head a wreath of exoneration and holiness.

Most poignant of all is Dionysis Kapsalis's 'The Suitcase' which
recreates Cavafy's last farewell with a heartbreaking irony worthy of
the elder poet:

Nor did anyone ask him why he needed
to take so many papers with him to hospital
since he would be up and back home again
in a few days.

A more knowing irony can be found in Angelos Parthenis's
'Cavafy Writes to Malanos' as the Alexandrian poet considers all the
'derivative material' his work has inspired:

Could it dull my Reputation? And could it even be
that my entire œuvre is no more than fad or pretext?

There are other, even more complex, transformations at work
here too. Ilias Margaris's melange of lines from several Cavafy
poems in 'Compiling Verses From Cavafy' presents an intriguing
tapestry, allowing stray phrases to reflect off each other, following
a tradition that goes back to the *cento* or 'patchwork quilt' of late
classical writers. To underscore these many intertextualities,
Nikolaou and Berengarten boldly embed quotations from a string
of notable English translations, including those of Keeley and
Sherrard. As Nikolaou points out in his additional online note, here

is 'a gathering of translations' to restitch – and repair – the original's 'assembly of excerpts and fragments'.

Margaris's lines begin with Cavafy's extravagantly-titled 1921 poem 'Melancholy of Jason, son of Kleander, poet in Commagene, A.D. 595', here quoted in the 2007 translation of Evangelos Sachperoglou. In another neat reflection, the volume continues with Nasos Vayenas's 'The Grammarian's Melancholy' in which Vayenas imagines a new character, Eudoxos the grammarian, 'stumbling upon | certain elegiac lines by Jason Kleander of Kommagini'. The poem's opening 'quotation' from Eudoxos summons up a parallel world where Cavafy's imaginary characters live and write alongside Vayenas's own:

> what we need is buoys to stay above water,
> words that inflate to keep us afloat in our own coracle...

History is similarly distorted in Yannis Voulis's 'From the Greek', the only poem in the anthology to echo Cavafy's trademark caesura line break. Voulis's poem is a version of Cavafy's 'Temethos, Antiochian, A.D. 400', relocating the original's eastern setting to Rome. Voulis also replaces Cavafy's eponymous Greek poet with 'the Roman consul/Quintus Lutatius Catlus', a Latin translator of the Greek epigrammatist Callimachus. This playful name immediately recalls the first-century BCE Roman poet Catullus who did indeed produce Latin versions of Callimachus. As Nikolaou and Berengarten translate:

> The rest of us might well pause
> to ponder certain alterations   which provide the key
> to this particular occupation   while also opening us
> to the heart of the translator.

In poems such as these, so skilfully rendered by Nikolaou and Berengarten's seasoned and sensitive hands, it seems as if the reader is inside a hall of mirrors where Cavafy is fractured into several parts at once – shrunk, grown, behind us and beyond us, a myriad of new, multi-faceted images. This small but perfectly-formed volume allows the heart of the translator and of the poet, both Greek and English, to open up between them.

Josephine Balmer

Bird-Made Language

Krystyna Miłobędzka, *Nothing More*, translated by Elżbieta
Wójcik-Leese, Arc Publications, 2013

Depending on a reader's knowledge of Polish poetry, the arrival of
Nothing More may seem like a miracle. A new voice, full of maturity,
nuance and daring seems to have arrived into the English language
out of nowhere. Miłobędzka, born 1932, is one of Poland's leading
poets. *Nothing More* is her first full-length book in English. It
samples her work from 1960 to 2008 and is more a condensation of
key concerns rather than a selection of individual poems.

In the preface, Miłobędzka describes her writing as the 'poetics
of jottings', and translator Wójcik-Leese correctly identifies
Miłobędzka's intent as 'keeping pace with what there *is*'. Like Emily
Dickinson, a named exemplar, she attempts to capture thought at its
most quicksilver put linear progress and narrative under pressure.
Unlike Emily Dickinson's hymn-like poems, however, the forms here
are mainly open, ranging from prose poem to lists and short lyrics.

The idea of poem-as-journal fits Miłobędzka's thematic focus:
Language, the Self and the World. Metaphors of family and lineage
are employed throughout: the social unit of the family, families of
words, grammatical units. This specificity precludes any risk of
vague generality.

Whereas the writings within one's personal journal usually
remain largely inert and of little interest linguistically, this is a book
of poems, where the energy of introspection is transmuted into a
style of verve and dynamism.

The reader is dropped into a swirling language from the first
piece: an untitled, small block of prose, short enough to bear
repeated reading but uncompromising. The landscape of the poem is

disorientating. The diction is sparse: pronouns, particles, articles, all in their correct positions, still seem to swarm and so the small units of grammar that form the building blocks of syntax are freed.

How does a reader orientate herself? This *how* is the question at the heart of this collection and the source of its unsettling power. Wójcik-Leese quotes Miłobędzka in the preface as saying there is 'nothing more important, more tender and mysterious than prepositions'. Interesting to observe the 'nothing more' here, mirroring the title of the collection. The collection as a whole can be read as one large preposition of sorts, with the reader confronted with his or her own desire for systemising and categorising.

The sensory content of these poems intrigues as it disorientates and a picture begins to form once considered long enough. Other categories of diction begin to come into focus, both noun and verb. Sign. Attempt. Swoop. Stab. Sprawled. Flutters. Utter. Sign. Feathery. By the time we reach the final word 'nest' we feel we are in the presence of a bird-like creature, or a real bird-made language.

This movement continues into the second and third poems in the collection. The poems have been gathered in a coherent manner and correspondences and associations begin to form over differing distances in the collection. The majority of pieces in this volume are untitled and this aids and invites the reader to travel across the pages. Fruitful associations can be made by reading this way. Recursive in theme, but restless in form and style, the disjointed and dislocated language and stitched effect result, paradoxically, in a cumulative tapestry. The many-angled approach, shifting perspectives and impressionistic touches may seem snatched and jotted when reading any one piece in isolation, but as with much poetry termed 'difficult', the longer the work is dwelt with, the more it begins to give up its deeper meanings and rhythms.

Rather than term it a stream of consciousness, it may be

more helpful to describe it as a meditation on the space between consciousness and speech. At times there are attempts to return even further, to a pre-linguistic state, and a confidence in communication is uncovered as language is questioned.

The fact that these poems are translations intensifies this questioning of language, self and the world. The themes are being worked out in two different musics, Polish and English. Arc Publications' usual practice of dual translation allows another set of questions to be asked. Do the forms match, for example? After choosing an enjambed line over the prose form of the Polish in the second two poems in the collection, 'House' and 'Quite Constricted...', Wójcik-Leese maintains the formal look of the poems almost to the line in the remainder of the collection, but inserts spatial buffers and blanks from time to time. She acknowledges this in her preface as a risk that aims to convey the instability of the Polish. I do not read Polish, so cannot judge in relation to this claim, but as poems themselves the practice strikes me as successful, as unsettled movement and energy are both everywhere evident. Robert Mihinnick in his introduction is right to call them more collaborations than translations, the result of a sympathetic partnership between Miłobędzka and Wójcik-Leese. As language itself is the liminal space being examined, the osmotic barrier through which feeling becomes thought and vice versa, even the physical fact of these poems being printed in dual translation deepens the thematic concerns. It reminds us that these concerns have also been explored in another language. I say 'have also' rather than 'were initially' as Wójcik-Leese is quite present in the English versions, as the process of translation is so closely aligned itself with so many of the key concerns in the book:

It makes two signs, vehement, ready for the uprush...

The first poem in *Nothing More* begins with a question: what is *It?* The final poem in the collection begins with the simplest but most profound of affirmative statements: *I am.* At heart *Nothing More* undertakes to articulate a precisely felt investigation into our perceived unity of self, and how we place language in service to this task to narrate our lives. Miłobędzka's work attests to the richer, more daunting prospect when we consider the actual disjointedness, speed and flow of one's thoughts, feelings and perceptions, especially in extreme states. This is a collection that not only attempts to track or map feeling becoming thought becoming language but also the opposite direction language>thought>feeling. This is the deeper rhythmic back-and-forth pulse at play here, and is ably and honestly translated in this edition.

Edwin Kelly

AGNÈS AGBOTON is an author from Benin now living in Barcelona, who writes in both her native Gen as well as in Spanish and Catalan. Earlier translations of her poems have appeared in *Wasafiri* and in the anthology *The World Record* (Bloodaxe).

ANA LUISA AMARAL is considered to be one of the foremost Portuguese poets of her day. She published her first collection of poems *Minha Senhora de Quê* in 1990, and has since published many more, along with plays, children's literature, a novel and translations from English.

FASIKA AYALEW works as an editor and writer for an English-language magazine called *Welcome to Addis* and is planning a book about the late poet laureate Tsegaye Gebre Medhin. Her next collection of poems is called *Longing*.

ALICIA AZA is a lawyer and a poet from Madrid. She has published three books: *El Libro de los árboles* (2010) which was a finalist for the Andalusia Critics award and was published also in a French translation; *El Viaje del invierno* (2011) which won the Rosalia de Castro International Poetry award and *Las Huellas fértiles* (2014).

RACHEL TZVIA BACK is a poet, translator and professor of literature. Her newest translation collection is *On the Surface of Silence: The Last Poems of Lea Goldberg* (2017). Her previous collection, *In the Illuminated Dark: Selected Poems of Tuvia Ruebner*, was a finalist for National Translation Award in Poetry (2015).

JOSEPHINE BALMER is a poet, translator and former Reviews Editor of *MPT*. Her most recent collection is *The Word for Sorrow* (Salt 2009 & 2013). Her study of classical translation and poetic versioning, *Piecing Together the Fragments*, was published by OUP in 2013.

JOSHUA BARLEY is a student of Modern Greek literature at King's College, London. Following a degree in Classics, he lived in Athens for two years and worked as a freelance translator. His translations have appeared at the 1st Athens World Poetry Festival and in *POEM* magazine.

ISRAEL BAR-KOHAV is a poet and a psychologist. The author of 12 books of poetry, Bar-Kohav's 2010 collection *Selected Poems 1975–2010*, published in the classics series of the Bialik Institute, places him among the first rank of contemporary poets of Israel.

CHRIS BECKETT's translation of poems by Bewketu Seyoum, *In Search of Fat*, was published by Flipped Eye in 2012 and his second collection of poems, *Ethiopia Boy*, came out from Carcanet/OxfordPoets in 2013. His collaboration with the Japanese artist and sculptor Isao Miura, *Sketches from the Poem Road*, was short-listed for the Ted Hughes Award earlier this year.

NORA BOSSONG, born in 1982, went to university in Berlin, Leipzig and Rome, and has published poems, novels and essays. Her latest publication is the novel *36.9°*.

RECAREDO SILEBO BOTURU was born in Baresó in 1979. He is a poet, playwright, narrator, essayist, actor, and theatre director from Equatorial Guinea.

CHARLES CANTALUPO has translated two books of poetry by Reesom Haile, *We Have Our Voice* and *We Invented the Wheel*. A new book of his poetry, *Where War Was – Poems and Translations of Poems from Eritrea* is published in 2016.

STEPHEN CAPUS was born in Swansea and studied Russian at the University of Birmingham and the School of Slavonic and East European Studies in London. His translation of the Hungarian poet Miklós Radnóti's *Letter to my Wife* was included in *Centres of Cataclysm*, published by Bloodaxe Books in 2016.

GEET CHATURVEDI is a noted Hindi poet and novelist. He has published six books, including two collections of six novellas: *Savant Aunty Ki Ladkiyan* and *Pink Slip Daddy*, and two collections of poetry. He was awarded the Bharat Bhushan Agrawal Award for poetry and the Krishna Pratap Award for fiction.

GEORGINA COLLINS is a Lecturer in Translation Studies at the University of Warwick and also works as a freelance translator. Her research focuses on the translation of Francophone African literature, with a special interest in women writers from Senegal.

TADEUSZ DĄBROWSKI (b. 1979) is a poet, essayist and critic. He has published six volumes of poetry and he has been published in many journals in Poland and abroad. He has received numerous awards and was shortlisted for NIKE in 2010, the most important Polish literary award. He lives in Gdańsk on the Baltic Coast of Poland.

JANE DRAYCOTT's most recent collection *Over* (Carcanet) was shortlisted for the 2009 T S Eliot Prize. She has been nominated three times for the Forward Prize for Poetry, and her first two full collections *Prince Rupert's Drop* and *The Night Tree* (Carcanet/ OxfordPoets) were both Poetry Book Society Recommendations.

INUA ELLAMS was born in Nigeria in 1984 and is an internationally touring poet, playwright, performer, graphic artist & designer. He has published three pamphlets of poetry *Candy Coated Unicorns and Converse All Stars*, *Thirteen Fairy Negro Tales* and *The Wire-Headed Heathen*.

IAIN GALBRAITH's poems have appeared in *Poetry Review*, *PN Review*, *TLS*, and many other books and journals. His book-length poetry translations include Jan Wagner's *Self-portrait with a Swarm of Bees* (2015), which won the Popescu European Poetry Translation Prize.

MICHALIS GANÁS (b. 1944) is one of the most distinguished poets and lyricists in Greece. He has won the State Prize for Poetry and his lyrics have been set to music by many composers, including Mikis Theodorakis. He has lived and worked in Athens since 1962.

CHEGE GĨTHIORA is Senior Lecturer at the University of London, SOAS. A linguist by training, he is widely published in Gĩkũyũ, Swahili, and English, and has translated Swahili poetry into Spanish.

GĨTAHĨ GĨTĨTĨ is a critic, poet and professor of English, Film and Media Studies, Africana Studies, and Comparative Literature at the University of Rhode Island. He is widely published in scholarly texts covering Africa, the African diaspora, and postcolonial studies.

ANITA GOPALAN is a translator and an artist. She was awarded the 2016 PEN/Heim Translation Fund Grant for her English translation of Hindi novel *Simsim* by Geet Chaturvedi.

HAFEZ (or Hafiz) is one of the most celebrated of Persian mystic poets, thriving alongside such towering figures as Rumi and Saadi. Interpreted variously as ardent mystic and lover, this extraordinary fourteenth-century poet fused earthly and divine love in ways that still resonate with general and spiritual readers alike.

REESOM HAILE's first collection of Tigrinya poetry won the Raimok prize, Eritrea's highest award for literature. He published two other books of poetry, translated by Charles Cantalupo and published by Red Sea Press – *We Have Our Voice* (2000) and *We Invented the Wheel* (2002) before he died in 2003.

SUSANNE HÖBEL is a translator of English literature into German. She has translated works by Nadine Gordimer, John Updike, William Faulkner, Graham Swift among others, and lives in Lewes, East Sussex.

MICHELE HUTCHISON was educated at UEA, Cambridge, and Lyon universities and worked as an editor for many years before becoming a full-time translator. She has translated poetry by various poets and novels by Ilja Leonard Pfeijffer, Tom Lanoye and Esther Gerritsen amongst others.

NORA IUGA was born in 1931 in Romania. Between 1971 and 1978, under the accusation that her work disseminated 'morbid eroticism' and would have a bad influence on the young generation, Iuga was banned by the communist censors from publishing fiction and poetry. Since then, she has published 15 collections of poems and seven books of prose.

MARGARET JULL COSTA has been a literary translator for nearly thirty years and has translated novelists such as Eça de Queiroz, José Saramago, Javier Marías and Teolinda Gersão, as well as poets such as Sophia de Mello Breyner Andresen and Ana Luísa Amaral.

J. KATES is a poet and literary translator who lives in Fitzwilliam, New Hampshire.

LISA KATZ is the translator of *Look There: Poems by Agi Mishol* (Graywolf); *Approaching You in English: Poems by Admiel Kosman* (with Shlomit Naim-Naor, Zephyr); *Late Beauty: Poems by Tuvia Ruebner* (with Shahar Bram, Zephyr). She edits the Israeli pages of the Rotterdam Poetry International web site.

EDWIN KELLY (@etakelly) lives in Dublin where he works as a Primary School teacher. His poems and translations have appeared in journals in the UK and Ireland. His experimental translation of Julian of Norwich *And After This I Saw* is published by Gatehouse Press.

ADMIEL KOSMAN is a prolific Israeli poet and postmodern scholar of traditional Jewish texts based in Berlin where he is tenured professor of Religious and Jewish Studies at Potsdam University, and academic director of the Abraham Geiger Reform Rabbinical Seminary.

ANTONIA LLOYD-JONES translates the work of two Polish poets: Tadeusz Dąbrowski, and – no relation – Krystyna Dąbrowska. She is currently co-chair of the UK Translators Association.

DIANA MANOLE is a poet and playwright, whose books include *Angel with a Canadian Visa* (2011), *Oh, That's Too Much!* (2000), *Evening Habits* (1998), and *Love on the Elevator* (1997). *B & W* is forthcoming in a dual-language edition from Tracus Arte, Bucharest.

JOYCE MANSOUR was a British-born francophone poet who grew up in Egypt. Her mother and husband died in her youth. She and her second husband moved to Paris where she developed a close friendship with André Breton who helped her publish her surrealist poetry.

CAROL MARTIN-SPERRY is a French literary translator who worked on the screenplays of Jean Cocteau. She has been a bilingual couples and sex therapist for the last 30 years and Fellow of the British Association for Counselling and Psychotherapy.

ZEWDU MILIKIT MEKONNEN was born in 1955. He has written many articles on education in Ethiopia and won prizes for his poems and short stories. His latest poetry collection is *Manew Yetetabat* (Who is it she suckles?). He lives in Gondar with his family and teaches at the Gondar Teachers College.

CHERYL MOSKOWITZ is a US-born poet and novelist, now living in London. She has been producing translations of Bewketu's work since 2007 when she spent some time in Ethiopia and was introduced to his writing.

MARIO PETRUCCI has translated modern and classical authors, including Montale, Neruda and Catullus. *Heavy Water: a poem for Chernobyl* (Enitharmon, 2004) secured the Daily Telegraph/Arvon Prize and was the basis of a celebrated film by Seventh Art Productions. Petrucci has been resident poet at BBC Radio 3 and the Imperial War Museum; he was recently shortlisted for the Ted Hughes Award.

ALFRED SCHAFFER was born in 1973 and grew up in The Hague, the son of a Limburger and an Aruban. In 1996, he moved to Cape Town, South Africa to continue his studies. He is the author of five poetry collections and has won numerous prizes including the prestigious Awater poetry prize.

LAWRENCE SCHIMEL is an author and translator living in Madrid. His most recent book in English is the poetry collection *Deleted Names* (A Midsummer Night's Press) and in Spanish, a collection of 100 microfiction *Una barba para dos* (Dos Bigotes).

MAME SECK MBACKÉ was born in Gossas, Senegal in 1947. She has written five collections of poetry, a short story, play and a novel and has won awards for her work, including the Premier Prix de Poésie from the Senegalese Ministry of Culture. She writes in both French and Wolof.

BEWKETU SEYOUM was born in 1980 and grew up in Gojam, Ethiopia. He studied Psychology at Addis Ababa University and has published six collections of poetry as well as stories, novels and essays. He has performed his poetry in London and New York and was the International Writing Fellow at Brown University for the academic year 2015–16.

DAVID SHOOK is Editorial Director at Phoneme Media. He grew up in Mexico City before studying endangered languages in Oklahoma and poetry at Oxford. His collection of poetry *Our Obsidian Tongues* was long-listed for the International Dylan Thomas Prize in 2013.

N.S. SIGOGO (1932–2008) is widely acknowledged as the most significant writer in siNdebele, the language of the minority ethnic group of southern Zimbabwe.

ADAM J. SORKIN is a translator of contemporary Romanian literature. He has published more than fifty books, most recently, in 2014, Marta Petreu's *The Book of Anger*, and Mihail Gălățanu's *The Starry Womb* (with co-translators). Sorkin is Distinguished Professor of English, Penn State Brandywine.

ALEMU TEBEJE is an Ethiopian journalist, poet and web-campaigner based in London. His poems have been published in the anthologies *Forever Spoken* and *No Serenity Here*, featuring 26 poets from 12 African countries. His website is www.debteraw.com

EMANUEL TEGENE was born in Ethiopia in 1985 and trained at the Alle School of Fine Arts and Design. He began his career in 2009 as a cartoonist for Saloon Ethiopia. He has exhibited his work a number of times: in 2014 he took part in the *Upcoming Art of Ethiopia* at the Sheraton Addis.

JAN WAGNER is a poet, essayist and translator of British and American poetry. He has published six volumes of poetry and his *Selbstporträt mit Bienenschwarm* (Self-portrait with a Swarm of Bees), his Selected Poems, was published in 2016. Jan Wagner has received numerous awards, including the Friedrich Hölderlin Prize (2011), the Mörike Prize (2015) and the Leipzig Book Fair Prize (2015).

BEDILU WAKJIRA is assistant professor of language and literature at Addis Ababa University. He is also well known for his outspoken articles in the Ethiopian press on social and political issues. He has published short stories, essays and three collections of poetry including *Fekat Nafeqiwoch* (Those who long for spring) and *Yetesfa Kitbat* (The Hope Vaccine).

STEPHEN WALSH is Head of the English Department at Christ's Hospital school in Sussex, England. He is the author of *Heartache Spoken Here* and *Faithful Departures* (Viking-Penguin Books).